A Guide to the Realms of Light

A *Guide* to the Realms of *Light*

Spiritual Teachings
From an Ascended Master Channeled by

Rt. Rev. Carole Mary Phelan

Terra Nova
Publishing LLC

Simi Valley, CA

Copyright © 2011 by C. M. Phelan

Terra Nova Publishing LLC
543 Country Club Drive, #B-301
Simi Valley, CA 93065
www.terranovapublishingllc.com

Printed in the United States of America

ISBN: 978-0-9837786-0-8

First Printing 2011

Cover Photo: Lewis Lagrell
Cover and Interior Design: Creative Publishing Book Design

Acknowledgement

This work is dedicated to my beloved husband, Christopher Phelan, without whose loving support, wisdom, faith and, maybe above all, patience I would never have undertaken, let alone completed this task.

Through the years he has taught me to have faith in myself, confidence in my abilities, and to finally accept that I am indeed a Child of God.

I, therefore, take this opportunity to thank him for his love and his guidance, and for not giving up on a very stubborn Capricorn.

I must also thank my teachers along the Way, and they know who they are. They opened many channels of learning to me, and helped me to open my eyes and unstop my ears.

Nor can I fail to thank my dear son, Colin, for always being there when I need him, even though I believe he sometimes thinks his mother is a little "flaky".

Lastly, but certainly by no means least, I must give thanks to Gezala and the Magic Circle for choosing me to be their channel for these teachings, for the love they expressed to me, and for the opportunity to grow a little more in wisdom. I promise them to Work, Pray and Meditate.

Book I

"And Gezala Said...."

Introduction

Gezala first made his appearance in my life on a brisk November day immediately after my morning meditation. His first contact was through what is generally known as 'automatic writing', although I prefer to call it spiritual writing.

At this first meeting he did not identify himself, and his first communication was very short. It was almost as though I was being tested for an assignment, or at least was on probation. However, after several more short lectures, I apparently passed my test and the formal introduction ensued, followed by longer teachings.

Having told me his name, Gezala informed me that he was one of ten teachers who form a group known as The Magic Circle. These teachers, chosen to participate in The Magic Circle because of their ability to teach and communicate the ancient wisdoms, are drawn from all corners of the Universe and from all ages. As each member of the Circle has a different area of "expertise", more than one of them might connect with the human channel as the need arose.

Gezala's particular talent was his ability to communicate through spiritual writing. As my assignment in this incarnation is to write, he was chosen to make the initial contact with me. He further told me that if the Circle decided it could do some verbal channeling to individuals or groups, another member of the Circle would be my contact. And I should mention that at a later date I was contacted by a lady of Indian heritage, and did do a small amount of verbal channeling for a limited number of people who came to me for help. However, it was made clear that my main assignment is to write, and therefore Gezala remains my principal contact in the Circle. He added that while he would be the one to actually speak with me, the remaining members of the group would be doing their part by focusing supportive energy while he worked with me.

It transpired that Gezala had more than one way of communicating. Initially our work together was in the form of "lectures", straightforward narratives. But as I became more comfortable with him, Gezala turned to other formats – poems, affirmations, meditations, and what I could only think of as psalms. While Gezala used these methods concurrently and on an ad hoc basis, I have divided them into separate sections in this book so as not to confuse the reader.

I find Gezala to be a kind, gentle and patient teacher. I am learning much from him and work every day to live my life in accordance with those teachings. His watchword is Work, Pray, Meditate, and I am seeking to emulate him.

I thought long and hard about publishing these teachings. Were they for me only? Was that a selfish attitude? Were there others who would be helped by these words? Would I be considered a crank or even a "devil worshipper" if I "went public"? Then I remembered that my assignment is to write, write, write. So here are the teachings of Gezala. For those who have eyes to see and ears to hear, I pray they will find what they seek in these pages. For those who have not yet reached that joyous state, Gezala, The Magic Circle and I bless them, and pray that they too one day will see and hear.

Carole Mary Phelan

Gezala's Teachings

There is little needs to be said for these teachings; they speak for themselves. I have transcribed them exactly as they were "dictated". I have not changed a word or, as far as I know, a comma or a period. Nor have I tried to interpret anything; I leave it to each reader to interpret these words as seems right to them.

All I can add is that if the reader is prepared to follow the Path of Work, Prayer and Meditation, all will be made clear.

I

How does the child become Man; how does the Man become God? Meditation, prayer and waiting upon the Lord – these are the tools of growth and only by their constant serious application can growth be achieved.

While you create your own Universe, you have to constantly recreate that Universe because your desires change as you grow. As you grow, the desires of your heart become more mature; you put aside the childish things and seek to find and experience the things of the mature One.

Why do you take so long to see that which is before you? You, and only you, can create those things you need, but with adulthood you recognize that the things **you** need must also benefit Mankind, and you must open yourselves to the recognition of what you can do to benefit Mankind through your actions. You are indeed your brother's keeper because your brother is as yourselves. Therefore you must do those things that are for your brother's good. Only in this way will you achieve those things that are for your good.

II

The body now is the expression of our individual human personality. But when all have realized the Divine Impersonality, this individual expression will no longer be needed and the Glory of the Spirit will manifest itself, needing no outer cloak to cover it. In that day you will once again emerge as Spirit, as Thought. The atoms that compose your human body will disintegrate, and you will manifest bodiless as Pure Thought – Immortal, Invisible, but GOD.

To that end, my brothers, pray and meditate that the day of Divine Impersonality may come to you; that the Keys of the Kingdom – Wisdom, Love and Power – may be put into your hands; that you will divest yourselves of your outer garments and reascend to Heaven – the Unity of the Divine Impersonality – as the Pure Thought and Spirit you once were, so that all powers and principalities may pass away save only the Kingdom of Heaven.

I salute the Divine Impersonality within you all and command you in the Name of the Supreme Being "Come forth from your shell and glorify Him who directs us all".

III

The Perfection of God is dependent upon the Perfection of each entity in His Creation. Until everything within that Creation has grown to perfection, God cannot express His full Perfection.

You must so grow, so spiritually advance towards your goal that the Perfected God shines forth. You must so perfect your planet, and all the elements of Creation, that it too will reflect the Perfected God, and all the units of His Creation will be manifested through the Holy Trinity of Wisdom, Love and Power. For from Wisdom will come the understanding of Love, and from the manifestation of Love will come the greatest Power in Creation – the Power of Perfection, the Perfected God. And to achieve that Perfected God each element must be perfect. Remember that at any moment you are perfect for that moment, but the perfection of the next moment is a step forward on the spiritual path. Time is the steps you take on that path – moment to moment a step nearer the Perfected God.

To be perfect, God needs each and every element of His Creation perfected – God needs a perfected YOU. Be ye, therefore, perfect even as your Father in Heaven is Perfect. Your level of Perfection is God's level of Perfection. Therefore work to be fully Perfect in all things. Work to be Pure Thought and Spirit that all things may come into Unity – the Unity of Perfection, the Perfected God.

IV

Dear Brothers in Christ, the Light has come to shine upon Mankind again, to fill all hearts with the Love and Knowledge of our Creator, if those hearts will be open to Him. The Three-Fold Flame of Light* must touch your three-fold nature. For you are indeed three – Body, the material perfection; Soul, the idea of Being, and Spirit, the Being of Being. In the Three-Fold Flame is the same manifestation, and the Flame and Man must be united.

Brethren, you have suffered long in darkness because you separated yourselves from your Creator. You buried your Godhead, but playacted the attributes of God, forgetting that you are a manifestation of His Creative Thinking. You took unto yourselves the power of making yourselves. But now you must return from whence you came, remembering that you are a part of God – His

---

The Three-Fold Flame of Light is the subject of a very ancient meditation, and is reproduced in the meditation section of this book for purposes of clarification only, and not by Gezala's dictation.

Idea, His Manifestation. And when you return to Him, He will restore to you all that you have lost – all Powers, all Knowledge, all Love, all Wisdom.

You have never really been separated from Him because He will not leave you, but you have told yourselves you are separate. But now you must know it is not so. God is One with His Manifestation, and has again sent His Light to show you the way. Become part of it; embody its attributes and you shall become as gods – an attribute of God that He created to bring His Creation into the Perfectability towards which it is growing. The Light is on the Path, Brothers. Follow its Rays, bathe in its Radiance, and become the Light of God.

V

The Temple of the Spirit must be built by the Spirit of Man. God has caused to well up in many the desire for a greater knowledge of Himself and of the Universe. Each day more and more seek to know of Wisdom, Power and Love, and with the burning of each desire, more radiance of the Light is shed on the Path. "Seek and ye shall find." All that has prevented you finding is the blindness of your eyes. Open your Eye and you will see all Knowledge. Open your Heart and you will have all Understanding. Open your Mind and you will have all Power. Knowledge, Understanding, Power – the Holy Trinity of Wisdom, Love and Power. The Christ of Wisdom – Buddha – has already visited you. The Christ of Love – Jesus of Nazareth- has already visited you. And the invitation has gone forth to the Christ of Power, for he will come with Peace and in the fullness of Peace – Peace within and quietness – is the Power. For in Peace you will find all things and know all things.

By tuning into the peace of your inner kingdom you will find the quiet in the eye of the storm that will enable you to meditate on all things and hear in the stillness the quiet voice of knowingness answer you. For knowledge is not a loud braying voice, but a strong quiet certainty – a full acceptance that you have joined your mind with the All-Mind and have drawn from the Universal Knowledge.

Therefore, Brethren, seek the stillness of the Heart, the quietude of the Mind and the peace of the Spirit, for in that Peace shall the everlasting Temple of God be built and blaze forth forever the Light of the World.

Walk in Peace and the Peace of God be with you.

VI

Dear Brethren, the Word of God speaks through many mouths – through the tree putting forth new shoots as it comes to the rebirth of Spring; through the clearness of the sky as it blazes with the light of the sun (the Light of the Son); through the joy and exaltation of a newborn babe, a Soul returned to the Earth plane with another opportunity to serve the Light of the World.

You must all accept these times of rebirth; to each of you is given the seasons of Life. In Spring you are reborn, recreated, a new channel for the Living God. You sow seeds, you create new thoughts and, through your thoughts, new worlds. In Summer you see the seeds come to flower, the fruits of your labors blazoning forth a paean of joy to their Creator. In Autumn you gather the rewards of your work and see your efforts come to full result. And then comes the Winter of seeming death, and you sleep and renew your spirits for the new Spring.

Spring and Youth; Summer and Young Adulthood; Autumn and Maturity; Winter and Old Age and Death. The cycle of birth and rebirth, death and reincarnation. And through the ages you have known this cycle. You have used these seasons of evolution to bring you to the Perfection of your Godhead. And now your labors are bearing fruit. You have seen your youthful Spring when the seeds were sown, and then you forgot them. They lay in the ground to germinate and you spent your time in youthful pursuits, forgetful of the planted seeds. You have seen your Summer when the seeds flowered and the gardens and lands of your souls saw the beauty that could be yours. But to achieve and keep that beauty meant that you had to labor in the fields, and surely the sunny days of Summer should not be wasted in labor, but should be enjoyed in pleasures? And you have seen the Autumn when the harvest was ready – the truths and perfections of the Divine were ready for your plucking, but where were the harvesters? Your Divine Creator showed you His Bounty and you could have shared His Godhead and known you were One with Him. But this would have meant turning your backs on earthly pleasures, pleasures that satisfied only the material nature of your being. And so you came to the Winter of Death. The earthly things you had pursued were taken away from you, and you slept.

O my brothers, do not let this be an empty sleep. While you sleep, let the dreams that pass through you awaken you to the full knowledge and realization of your Godhead. Know without doubt that you are One with God – that He is in you and you are in Him. As the new Spring of your Being approaches lay hold on your Soul and vow to bring it through the seasons to the fullness that awaits you.

Take to yourself the Trinity of Rebirth – Work, Pray, Meditate, and through **this** Trinity bring to pass the Trinity of the Perfected God – Love, Wisdom, Power, these three, and the greatest is still Love. For from the wellspring of Love will come the Power and the Wisdom. The Trinity of Rebirth; the Trinity of the Perfected God. Build the path between them, brothers, and walk in the Light.

The radiance of God be on you, that the Spring of your rebirth will lead you to the Harvest of Autumn, so that the Winter of Death may pass away. Spring, Summer, Autumn – the Trinity of Life Everlasting.

In the Name of the Father, Son and Holy Spirit, God be with you.

VII

The flowers of the field show forth the glory of our God in all His Perfection, for at the moment of their full blooming they are Perfect as He intended them to be.

You too may be Perfect as you come into the full bloom of your being. As the flowers of the field, God has chosen for each of His Attributes a peak of Perfection, a blueprint of the Perfected Attribute that contributes to the Perfected God.

You must go within yourselves to the junction of Self and Impersonal Self to read that blueprint. You already know that God is within you, that you and God are One. You know that it is possible for you to know all things as He does, if you accept that union with your Godself. So, in attaining that state you can know what you are to be and you can see the paths that you must walk to achieve that Perfection.

But the most important path you must walk at any time is that of Acceptance – acceptance of what you are, acceptance of your place in life, acceptance of your work, your friends, your home. Acceptance of, not complacency with, nor a state of apathy, but true acceptance. Remember that each state of being is perfect for that moment. Therefore you must fully accept the perfection of any one moment before you can move on to the perfection of the next moment, before you can achieve the next step in your walk towards the All Perfect, the Perfected Perfection of your reunion with your Godhead. "Ye are gods in the making." "Ye are little less than the angels, and it does not yet appear what ye shall be." Why does it not yet appear what you shall be? Because until you come near to the Perfected Perfection, God is not yet Perfect. He can only show you what you will be when you show Him what you can be.

Why are you in work that dissatisfies you? Because there is knowledge and power that you have not yet awakened that you could use in that work which would make it completely satisfactory. Why do so many of your plans and projects go awry?

Because you are using them for less than perfect reasons – for your own perfection rather than God's. Why are your friends not really those with whom you feel in harmony? Because those friends you have can awaken in you knowledge of your own imperfections.

Examine yourself. Examine every aspect of your life. Ask yourself – the I AM of you – where it is imperfect, and seek through work, prayer and meditation for its perfecting. Ask that the Light of Lights shine on you, and in that Light you will see the Imperfect and the Perfect it will become. Know that the Perfected God awaits you and holds out His Hands to you, seeking in Love the union that once was.

Return to your Perfection that the Universe may be perfected.

The time is fast approaching for the coming of the Prince of Peace, when Love shall indeed fill all things. Wisdom and Love await now the Power of Peace, and when that Triumvirate is complete, God, Man and all Creation must be Perfect.

The time is running out, brothers. There is no more time for delay; no more time to take diversions away from the True Path. Work, pray and meditate. The hour is near when we shall be called on to serve in all Perfection.

Come, my brothers, let us take our journey to the peak. Let the Light of Christ Consciousness fill you and guide your steps to the Mountaintop of Godhead. You are the Lord's servants. Strive to serve Him in Perfection. Wisdom, Love and Power, your three guides and teachers, be with you. The Light of God be on you all the days of your Being. I salute the Eternal Brotherhood of God.

VIII

In the midst of life there is yet light, however dark the day. The Light will spread until it fills the earth, and the radiance of it will conquer the darkness. Fear not, my children, lo! the Light is breaking. Fear no more the darkness, but know you are the focal point for the Light. It spreads from you and returns to you, and you are the Light as the Light is you.

Stand in the Light, my children. Dance in the Light. Send forth your songs into the Light, and all shall be spread before you. Partake of the Lord's feast. Fill yourself with His nourishment, and never feel hunger again.

You are His and He is yours, and you and He are One.

Shalom, Shalom, Shalom

IX

Love is the key, the cornerstone. Without it the building cannot stand. Love – have ye love one for another. On this is all built, and without it nothing lasting is built.

I love you, love you one another. Support and sustain one another. Give heed to the needs of each other. Succor each other in times of trial.

Stand forth! The trumpet has sounded from the heights. Come unto Me and share My Joy. Peace and Joy shall be yours on the Morning Mountain. Scale the heights and stand upon the peak and all shall be made known.

In Perfect Knowledge is Perfect Understanding. In Perfect Understanding is Perfect Peace. In Perfect Peace is Perfect Love.

Hosanna hallelujah! Joy is come unto the earth. She shall sing and be glad.

X

God is coming to His people. He has sent His Light before Him, and they that bathe in the radiance of that Light shall shed the Glory of God on all Mankind. They will be given the tongues to speak and shall make way for the Lord. They will speak of the Holy Trinity of Wisdom, Love and Power, and shall bring to Mankind the Peace of Unity and Brotherhood.

XI

I said "Speak, Lord, for Thy servant heareth." And he said: "Write", and I asked "Lord, what shall I write?".

And He said: "Write of the goodness and the glory of God; write again that the earth is the Lord's and the fullness thereof. Where there has been darkness, behold, the Light shall shine. Where there has been hate, Love shall flow as the River of Life. There shall be abundance for all who serve the Highest, and He shall place His Mark of the Risen Christ on all who have died to the world, that they may be resurrected in Him."

Call on the Lord, my brethren. Call on the Highest that He may raise you to His Heights. Come before Him with rejoicing and gladness. For it is written that the Lord loves a joyful man. For in joy we touch the highest peaks of serenity and of peace. In joy we love one another as ourselves, and thereby achieve that vibration which takes us to the Perfection of the Perfected God.

Seek that Perfection, my brothers, and from that Height of Heights will come the Light that will create the millennium of Peace, Love, Harmony – the Trinity of Perfection.

XII

To those who seek an easy path, this will not point the Way. Nor, indeed, will they actually find an easy path. There is no such thing. But, there is a **simple** path.

The signposts are clearly spread before us. The instructions are clearly stated. The traveler who follows the signposts by way of the instructions will find the rough places made plain; will find support and courage for the journey, and will reach journey's end. But not easily. In fact, the plainer the way, the clearer the instructions, the more accurate the signposts, the harder the journey.

In other words, the more you know, the harder it becomes. It is easy to explain away digressions when one is ignorant. But how much more difficult to "get away" with those digressions when one knows the rules!

"Love thy neighbor as thyself." Easy, no? No!! How do you love yourself? Do you think yourself perfect, or do you view yourself "faults and all"? Or do you "hate" yourself because you do not see yourself fulfilling all your ideals?

To "love thy neighbor as thyself" first recognize and accept that you are both Children of God, both aspects of the Divine Expression. Your neighbor is yourself, you are your neighbor. "There is no separation in Divine Mind"...."We are One in the Spirit"....

not empty cliché, but accurate expressions of Beingness. Every being existing today, in whatever plane, in whatever form, is your neighbor. If you cannot love yourself **as you are,** you cannot love your neighbor. It has been written of two beings that they were "as two cherries on one stalk", but we are even closer than that. We are all one cherry on one stalk. We are all included in the 360 degrees of one circle.

Know this. Accept this. And you have begun to love your neighbor as yourself and taken the first step on the **simple** path.

XIII

This is the Truth of Truth, that for a man to know completeness he must bring about in his being the unification of Wisdom and Love.

When a man asks God to become One with him, God's Love will give to that being the Spirit of Divine Power, Love and Discipline, demonstrating an abundance of Life even greater than that found in the union of body and soul.

Because of the magnitude of the Holy Spirit, the power of that Spirit is poured forth into the universe, and raises the consciousness of Man through the awakening of his senses, both on the inner and outer planes, the spiritual and the material.

When a being is made aware that he can achieve complete oneness with God, he is ready to set out on the journey of evolution, and he begins the awakening of the spiritual centers within his beingness, raising the fire of the Kundalini.

As the flame of I AM grows and rises from the first chakra* to the seventh, Man becomes aware of his Oneness with God, and is filled with joy.

At the point marking the end of involution (physical incarnation) and the beginning of evolution, Man is in a state of ignorance, and his thoughts are confused and unsettled. But there is a spark of awareness beginning to grow in him; a need to set out on the path that will bring him eventually to the union of Love and Wisdom and the Oneness of God.

A being in a state of ignorance, in a state of becoming, should not be despised, because God has blessed him by making him aware that he can evolve to that Oneness.

XIV

Long ago when the land was new and Light still flooded the earth, Man in his glory stood at the peak of the angels and held them in his arms. They were his friends and companions, and joined him in his endeavors, giving him the Light of their Love and Wisdom. But Man grew gross in his opinion of his own wisdom, and decided he could stand alone.

"What need have I of angels," said he, "when I have my own mind and brain? There is nothing they can give me that I do not contain within myself."

And so Man cut himself off from his inspiration, and grew great in his own pride, and life became a time of trial, of trouble,

---

* The chakras are the seven spiritual centers in the body human

of back-breaking work. And Man said "Why has God punished me and left me in darkness?", forgetting that it was he himself who had cut off the Light and shut the door on his communication with the Highest.

And now, in his turmoil, Man has called again to God and asked to be delivered out of the darkness. And God has answered and said "You must make the decisions of yourself that will bring you back to union with Me. For you have shunned Love and Light, you have chosen to run after the matters of mind and body, and not the matters of Spirit. You seek the wealth on earth, not the wealth of Heaven. You lavish care and material goods on your bodies; you run after fools and mountebanks crying Master, Master, and fill your minds with the empty mouthings of those who wear the mask of gods. You shatter your beings with loud and raucous noise to cover your emptiness. But how many of you seek Me in the silence? In the still and quiet places of the earth shall you find me; in the sound of a child's laughter, in the song of praise trilled forth by a bird; in the stillness of a tree or flower after the wind has passed; in the silent blessings of the rain, in the benison of sleep and in the high places of earth – there am I found.

Rise up, O Man, and make your way to the high places. Seek Me on the mountain and I will come to you. The Light has shined on those who know the Way and will lead.

If one speaks to you in silence, hear him, for his is My Voice. But heed not those who shout my glory from the rooftops, for these are not of My Voice, but seek rather to bring that glory on themselves and call it their own. Those who truly know Me have no need to shout, for My Presence with them shines forth for all to see, and needs no advertising.

It was in the stillness of the evening and of the dawn that I spoke with Adam and he heard Me. The loud and raucous do not hear Me, for they are speaking too loudly themselves.

For you who have eyes to hear and ears to see, to know and comprehend the Light and the Silence, go within to your private room, and there I will await you. We will speak together in the Silence, and each will know the other's thought. In Love and unison will we sing, and the Light will flood the earth from our mouths.

I will hear when you call to Me, and if you work and truly seek Me, I will be there and we shall be One again.

Come forth, my children, out of the noise and strife, into the stillness and joy, and I shall give you radiant peace until the consummation of the worlds.

As it was, is now and evermore shall be. Selah. Amen."

XV

If you were to construct an element of work in terms of electricity, you would be using one of the building blocks of Creation. The work would, therefore, be filled with light, or rather Light, and would be no burden but, rather, a joy. Did not the Master say "Take my burden upon you and learn of Me, for My burden is Light"? Was He then saying that Creation is Light, that the only "burden" Man should bear is the Light? He further said "Ye are the Light of the World". If, then, Light is the creative force, and you are the Light of the World, you are then the creators of the world. You, and you only, have made the world as it is. But it would seem that you have reversed the Light and have tried to build with Darkness.

Wherever one looks in this world that you have created one sees war, strife, unrest, brother killing brother, black killing white, white killing black, ethnic group against ethnic group. You are systematically destroying the world you created. Profits are more important than the planet.

To make money, Man is steadily denuding the forests of the planet, so that the trees will no longer carry moisture to the earth, to feed and nourish it. The fruits and vegetables of the planet are being destroyed by chemicals. The animals of the planet are being slaughtered to extinction. The lakes, rivers and seas of the planet are being contaminated by chemicals so that the denizens of the waters are being poisoned and eliminated. Even the birds of the air are not safe – either killed by hunters or poisoned by pollution. Many people born into this planet during the last fifty years have never known how natural food really tastes. Either cigarettes have deadened their ability to taste or they eat only chemically produced or nurtured matter.

Why did Man, as Spirit, elect to create this earth and then withdraw the Light from it? Why is Man's heart so filled with envy and hatred, denying the Light entry to that heart? The struggle is indeed between Light and dark, and it must seem to many that the dark is winning.

But the Light can never be defeated. It may be unseen by many, but that is not because the Light has departed. Rather it is because their eyes are closed. Man has allowed himself to fall into that sleep of forgetfulness that blinds his eyes to the Light. You, Mankind, have forgotten that you are the Children of God. You, Mankind, have forgotten that you are the Bearers of the Light, that you **are** the Light.

Sleepers, awake!

To those who know the Light, who know they are the Light, let **your** Light so shine before men that it awakens them again to the knowledge of who and what they are. Maybe at this time you are a small scattered brotherhood, but throughout the history of this planet of your creation, great acts and changes have been wrought by a few. And the few has grown to many. There is no obstacle so great you cannot learn from it and conquer it. There is no avenue of work that the Light cannot be directed into. There is no house so divided it cannot again be united.

Out of the darkness comes the Light. Out of chaos comes order. Go forth in the knowledge that you are the bearer of order to tame the chaos.

Why do you tarry? There is no time to lose. Before the planet is destroyed, before its people are destroyed and this world explodes into empty nothingness, you must make your stand. Put on the whole armor of God and stand. Forget your human puniness. You are omniscient, omnipotent, none can withstand you. Rise up, O Men of God, go forth in the battle between the Light and the darkness, filled and surrounded by the Light, and you must prevail. Have no fear. The Light casts out fear. This Light that lighteth every man knows only perfect love, perfect trust and perfect peace. Never doubt that you are the Children of God. Never doubt that you are One with the Source and all creation.

Each act of destruction within your planet diminishes your human selves and can, if you let it, diminish your spiritual strength.

You cannot continue to walk this path of destruction. You must return fully, totally and completely to the Light. He that walks in the Light has eternal Life, and the death bell will never toll for him. Do not let the darkness seek to conquer the Light. Go forth in faith. Go forth in Love. Go forth in Peace. The Light is and always shall be **ALL**.

Pace Domini, Pace Filius, Pace Spiritus. Amin. So Be It.

XVI

Know this, that from the very soil the life force springs and moves upward to the Light. It seeks the Light because life cannot exist in darkness. Nor can it remain buried in the earth. It must manifest in Light and Air for it is of the Light and Air, of Power and Spirit, and thus it has been and will for ever be.

Out of the night comes the day, returning in its cycle to infuse Mankind with the Light and to give rest at eventide. All things must rest, plants, beasts and men. From rest comes strength and the Light demands strength. Out of the darkness of ignorance comes the Light of Knowledge, and to spread that Knowledge the being must be of the highest vibration. It can only be so by loving and respecting the body, the Temple of the Living God.

And so God gave darkness at night that the body might cease from the search for knowledge and the mind find ease. But there must not be darkness at noon, for at the twelfth hour the being – mind, soul and body – is at its peak.

Give wing to the thoughts that come from these sayings, for out of these thoughts shall come great knowledge of the Light.

Go in Peace, My Children. This time together is now ended, but when you have more need of my teachings, I will speak with you again.

Remember I am always near you. I love you as you love me, and together we will build the Hill of the Most High.

In pace domini. In nomine Spiritus Pater, Spiritus Filius, Spiritus Sanctus. Amen

Gezala's Affirmations

*T*o Gezala these Affirmations are strong foundations of his faith. To him they are the reaffirmation of that faith, and the daily reiteration of them provides the means of strengthening and cementing his belief.

He does not suggest that everyone necessarily adopt these particular Affirmations, but stresses the importance of each and every one of us making our own Affirmations, whether by adopting or adapting these examples, or by creating something completely personal. It is the act of making the Affirmation, not any particular set of words, that is important.

But the daily statement of the Affirmation must not become empty recitation. The words must be spoken, whether verbally or silently, with complete sincerity and in the steadfast knowledge that you make your Affirmation as a Child of God and as a channel of God in Action.

He further stresses that as one travels along the path of growth the content of one's Affirmations might well change as one's knowledge, understanding and degree of faith change and one's unbelief falls away – "Lord I believe, help Thou my unbelief." Therefore, one *should never hesitate to make these changes. This is not inconsistency or evidence of a "revolving door mind", but rather the recognition of one's growth and development. So take Gezala's Affirmations to your heart, and then seek your own Way.*

I

I Am the Body of God, the manifested evidence of the Presence. The Spirit of God creates all things, and uses me to perform them in the sight of Man. To know this is to know the Peace of God, for if God causes all how can there be ill-effects to disperse His Peace? I know that my Redeemer liveth, and manifests that Life through me. Therefore all that I need, all that I want of Good is mine. I have no fear of what I shall eat, what I shall drink, with what raiment I shall clothe my nakedness. I have no fear of taking care of all my needs. God is, therefore I AM. None can take this from me.

Life is lived from within, with the inner knowingness of the Presence as Father and the Christ as Master. With such a Father and such a Teacher how can life be lived other than to the fullest, without fear and in Perfect Peace.

God and I work as the One we are, to manifest all that embodies a full, balanced Spiritual Life, the needs to maintain a healthy physical body and the needs to maintain a perfecting Spiritual Being.

II

I cannot know fear, for I AM the master of my Being. I have set my path and step on it in True Faith. I KNOW. This is faith. To know all even if such knowledge does not physically manifest. To know I know is enough. When the manifestation of knowledge is needed it will appear, even as the Teacher when the student is ready.

The Light falls constantly and continuously on my Path, but I must clear the dazzle that blinds me from my eyes before I can see that Light and stand within it. I see each step as it is made clear, and as I advance on the Path my interpretation of the step I see will be clearer. Today I see as a child. Tomorrow – which will become and is my new Today – I will see and do as a Child of the Light. In infinite Wisdom it is given to me to manifest that which I can understand and through understanding express truly.

In Truth is my Knowledge. In Knowledge is my Understanding. In Understanding is my Faith. Lord, I believe; help Thou my unbelief.

Gezala's Poems

In using the blank verse format for some of his teachings, Gezala had two different ends in mind. Firstly, he feels that some people find poetry easier to handle than prose narrative, easier to remember and retain. Secondly, like the Nostradamus Prophecies, he chooses to put deeper, more esoteric truths into a format that takes work and study to decipher.

The poems can be taken purely at face value, or those who choose to do so can find deeper meanings, and maybe even prophecy. "For those who have eyes to see, let them see. For those who have ears to hear, let them hear."

God's Battlecry

Take my hand, thou failing one,
And together we will make a stand
For God and Truth and Righteousness;
For from this Trinity will come
The shining Light of Perfect God
To make Divine all things that worship Truth.
There is no separation in My World,
For I have made all things One,
United 'neath the Orb of Jove.
He who comes next will cap My Trinity
Of Wisdom, Love and Peace.
Give aid to Him that He may aid all Men.
Through Him will distrust's sword
Trust's mighty ploughshare yield,
And separation's spear, the pruning hook of Unity.
Gone will be the discords of this age,
And Perfect Wisdom, Peace and Love
Will light the three-fold flame of Christed Life
For all Mankind.
Gezala speaks to all who hear – Heed my words
    and bear your part;
Fulfill the task for which you came, and God will
    give you everlasting Light,
And call you blessed, that you may take your hallowed place
Within the Kingdom of the Gods.
So mote it be.

Union

God from who all blessings flow,
Grant me this of Thee to know,
That Thou and I are One indeed,
That hand in hand and step by step
We walk together to a promised end
That is no end but the beginning of
All Life that knows no end.
There is a Song we all shall sing,
There is a Song all joy shall bring,
The Song that says the Lord is come.
O welcome, Lord, unto Thy Home.
My heart is open, Lord, to Thee;
My mind has spread its doors to Thee,
And to my Soul Thou hast the key.
Lord, I have sung my song to Thee,
And asked Thee for Thy blessing, Lord.
The truth that cometh like a sword,
And severs me from all that was,
That shut me from the sight of Thee, the Light of Thee.
Now I stand within that Light;
That Light AM I as it is me;
For we are One, My Lord and I:
I AM He and He is me.

The Hill of God

There is a door that all men enter by
To take their walk unto the Hill of God.
A serpent Goat shall be its sign,
To set the feet of Man securely on the Path.
But Man, forgetting his Divinity, climbs spirally,
Not by the straight Path of the Cross.
From Goat to Crab must Man most surely make
    His Way
Straight from the Cross's foot unto its Head,
There to resume that shed Divinity.
Seven times twelve he walks,
A sum that brings him to the Trinity;
And seven Trinities he shall seek and find
That knows the Path to Perfect God.
Seven Trinities to make an eighth –
That of Divinity.

The Garden of Remembrance

Come to the Garden of Remembrance
Where all things live forever.
Here learn that nothing dies
But is a constant reminder of God's eternalness.
Our eyes long misted by the sights of earth
Do not see the lights and shadows, dimensions
Not of this world.
Come, wash your eyes with Christ's Pure Light,
(Some call Him Buddha, some Kahlil, Some Jesus,
    some Great Lord Krishna –
It matters not for this too is eternal,
A glowing orange peak reached by those who climb
    and seek,
Leaving the matters of the world behind)
And through their new glowing gaze see those who
    passed this way before
And those still yet to come.
Follow with these eyes the never-ending umbilical cord
That binds the generations fore and aft.
All are but aspects of the same family,
But some have passed to other planes and other
    lands
Other planets, one universe.
We too must walk and follow them, and reaching
    journey's end
Fold our hand into the Hand of God.

Look For Me

Go forth, O Soul, unto thy rest,

Returning to that God from whence you came.

Hold high the torch of Godhead,

And make it known to all who see.

Thine is this Path to tread, and thine alone.

Fear not to speak the things that thou dost know.

God is thy Judge, and He alone shall give thee words

That lift the hearts of Men,

Giving them knowledge and the Keys of Truth

To shape the Path to Him.

Out of thy mouth shall come the Sword of Life

To sever lie from Truth.

And none shall come between thy God and thee,

But He shall stand beside thee in the Way,

Showing the Path and making all things plain.

Hold high thy head; give utterance to God's word which
  now we speak,

And it shall come to pass as I have said, in His Golden Day,

Out of whose Hand the healing power shall come

To raise all Men to me.

Go now in peace, My Child, and take my Grace to
  Shield thee in this world of men.

Look for Me. I do not tarry long in coming.

My Christ

Comfort in sorrow;
Help in distress;
Rest in weariness;
Inspiration in despair;
Strength in weakness;
Truth in eternity –
This is **my Christ**, my Lord,
Who has lifted me from death to life
And will be my **SUN** for evermore.

The Voice

Out of nothingness a voice spoke,
And there was light and land and sea.
Out of nothingness a voice spoke,
And there was nourishment and beingness and Man.
From "no-thing-ness" came all that is,
And it is real and good.
For the voice that spoke from no-thing-ness
Put forth the Power of God.
There is no-thing that is not of Him,
For He is all that is.
And He is Man, and Man is Him,
And No-thing-ness is All.

Gezala's Psalms

Gezala explained the difference between his Poems and his Psalms this way. The Poems were another way of communicating with his human channels; the Psalms were his paean of praise to the Supreme Being, his Creator, his God.

As any reader of the Book of Psalms will recognize, Gezala's Psalm II is composed of verses taken from several of the Biblical Psalms (118:17-18; 138:7, 71:20; 18:5-7 and 16-17; 16:8-11; 49:15; 21:1-5) with some minor alterations in the words. Gezala's explanation for this is that as we are all One, and have access to all knowledge, we share all that ever was and is created, and this collection of verses, like David's, expresses his total and undying faith in redemption and salvation for all. He adds that this is also the explanation for more than one composer using the same melody, for scientists, in totally different parts of the world, making the same "discovery" at the same time; for more than one person having the same thought at the same time – things of which we have all had experience

As far as Gezala is concerned, there is no such thing as plagiarism; it is simply that we all have the ability to tap into all that ever was, is and will be.

~
I
~

I have stood upon the Mountain of the Lord and seen. I will see
again as it is given to me.

Lift me up, O Faith, that I may stand upon the peak and render
to the Cosmos all that it is due.

Let me stand on the Peak of Darien that nothing may be hidden.

Let me stand on the Peak of Ethos that all may be known.

Let me stand on the Peak of Domini that all may be spoken.

Let me stand on the Peak of Harmony that all may be shared.

Let me stand on the Peak of Agarn that all may be loved.

Glory to the Most High; Glory to the Son; Glory to the Spirit.

Amos, Amos, Amos

Hallelujah

---

*Peak of Darien: Darien is the central ruling principle of the sense consciousness
to do with the five senses, but at the same time consciously aware of the place of
spiritual judgment within this. In Hebrew numerology Darien translates to 5,
while in modern numerology it translates to 33, the number of the Holy Trinity.*

*Peak of Ethos: Ethos is the Greek equivalent of Emmanuel, and is concerned with
the moral nature or guiding beliefs and the Godself that is within us. Hebrew
numerology gives Ethos the value of 1. while its value in modern numerology is 22,
the number of the Father and the Son.*

*Peak of Domini: Domini is the name for a teacher or lecturer (in 18th century
Scotland, for example, a school master was called a dominie), therefore, one who
"speaks" and in this instance one who speaks truth.*

*Peak of Harmony: This, I think, is self-explanatory, in that if all live in harmony,
all that is good will be shared.*

*Peak of Agarn: This would appear to be a variant or alternative of the Greek word
Agape, meaning a spiritual love feast or communion.*

*Amos: Knowing affinity for or love of the natural forces of mind and body, which
are of the Most High through the Son in its expression.*

How are the mighty gathered, O Lord, to feed on Thee and Thy Works.

Lord, come again that Thine Own may know Thee.

Come to each and every one of us created from Thy splendid Chaos; created to garner love and joy; to bring comfort and solace where needed; to bring peace and tranquility; to bring again the Prince of Peace and Love.

Enter Thy Kingdom, Lord; Thy servant waits.

Dominum Pacifica

Heart of my heart, Lord of my life, praise and thanksgiving to Thee be my only song.

Teach me, O Lord, to praise Thy Name and show forth Thy goodness in my life.

I climb, O Lord, to the Peak of the Holy Mountain. Aid Thou my steps. I come, Lord, I come. Hold Thou my hand and I will enter into Glory. Amen, Amen, Amen.

I have done. The speech is ended for this time.

Hallelujah. Emmanuel has come again to Men.

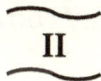

II

I shall not die, but live and declare the works of the Lord. The Lord has chastened me sore; but He hath not given me over unto death.

Dominum Pacifica: This means peace through our total expression of the Law of the Lord.

Though I walk in the midst of trouble, Thou wilt revive me; Thou shall stretch forth Thine hand against the wrath of mine enemies; Thy right hand shall save me.

Thou which hast shewed me great and sore troubles, shalt quicken me again, and shalt bring me up again from the depths of the earth.

The bands of the grave compassed me about; the snares of death prevented me. In my distress I called upon the Lord, and cried unto my God.

He heard my voice, out of His temple, and my cry came before Him, even into His ears.

Then the earth shook and trembled; the foundations of the hills moved and were shaken......

He sent from above, He took me, he drew me out of great waters. He delivered me from my strong enemy.

I have set the Lord always before me; because He is at my right hand I shall not be moved. Therefore my heart is glad, and my glory rejoiceth. My flesh also shall rest in hope.

For Thou wilt not leave my soul in the grave; neither wilt Thou suffer Thy Holy One to see corruption.

Thou wilt show me the path of life; in Thy Presence is fullness of joy; at Thy right hand are pleasures for evermore.

The king shall joy in Thy strength, O Lord, and in Thy salvation how greatly shall he rejoice......

Thou settest a crown of pure gold on his head. He asked life of Thee, and Thou gavest it him, even the length of days for ever and ever.

And his glory is great in Thy salvation; honor and majesty hast Thou laid upon him.

Gezala's Meditations

*G*ezala felt he could not too strongly stress the need for daily meditation. He looks on it as **the** door to growth, to development, to ever-increasing knowledge and understanding, to becoming ever-more aware of Oneness with the Living God.

He emphasized that there is no one way of meditating, that there are as many ways to meditate as there are people who meditate, and that no one way is better than another. The important factor is that each person should be completely comfortable with their choice of meditative activity. On the other hand, he stated there are some essentials that should be observed, which he laid out in the following seven steps:

First, physical comfort. If you can sit in the lotus position, do so, but it is not essential. It is more important to sit comfortably, and a perfectly acceptable position is described in the breathing exercise that appears on page 47 of this section.

Second, breathing. To control one's breathing is to demonstrate one's ability to control one's life, and a meditation should always be preceded by a breathing exercise. There are many such exercises, and the one described on page 47 is just a sample, although it is an extremely effective one.

Third, timing. If possible, your principal daily meditation should be at the same time and in the same place every day, as this builds up a growing edifice of spiritual energy in that place. But even if you cannot manage this, it is better to meditate when and where you can than to miss a daily meditation.

Fourth, concentration. In order to achieve the higher levels of meditation, you must empty your mind of all extraneous thoughts and **concentrate** on what you are doing. If such outside thoughts come into your mind, banish them immediately, and continue to **concentrate** on your meditation.

Fifth, guard against disappointment. Even the most advanced gurus cannot always achieve sustained meditations. The majority of people can achieve only four or five minutes of pure meditation at a time; the rest is contemplation of concepts offered by your Higher Self. But this too is good, and aids in spiritual growth.

Sixth, choice of individual or group meditation. For your own spiritual growth, you need your own daily individual meditation. Group meditation, particularly when it is for healing, can build a greater field of energy to be directed to those in need of help. But as group meditation is usually guided by a leader, it is once again mainly contemplation.

Seventh, silence. What you learn in your meditation is for you alone, and not for others. Keep these things to yourself and ponder them in your heart. If anything you learn is to be passed on, that will be made very clear to you. If you like to use music, candles or incense when you meditate, do so. They are not essential, but they can assist in achieving relaxation.

Example of a Pre-meditation Breathing Exercise

Sit comfortably with hands loosely in your lap, palms upwards, and eyes closed, and put your attention on your breathing. Do not attempt to change it in any way or to judge it in any way. Focus totally on your breathing.

Now, as you breathe in, focus your attention on your left nostril. As you breathe out, focus your attention on your right nostril. Take no physical action of any kind. Simply focus your attention on your left nostril as you breathe in and your right nostril as you breathe out.

When you are comfortable with this rhythm, add this dimension: As you breathe in with your attention on your left nostril, visualize (or imagine) a stream of pure golden white light flowing into you through your left nostril. See the breath entering your being in this steady stream of pure golden white light. Be aware the breath of life is entering your being through the light.

As you breathe out with your attention on your right nostril, visualize the golden white light leaving your nostril in a sparkling fountain of light, returning to the universe.

Be aware that as the Light passes through your being it is cleansing it of all impurities, all that is non-optimum, leaving you radiant., relaxed, glowing with beauty.

When you are ready, take three deep breaths and expel them gently through your nostrils to end this exercise. You are now ready for your meditation.

~ I ~

A LIGHT MEDITATION

We would now have you picture in your imagination, at arm's length, on the right side of your head, a small spark of light. Now, mentally visualize that spark of light coming forward, still at arm's length, to directly in front of your forehead. Bring it towards you and place it in the center of your forehead. Feel it there, see it there. Now bring the light into your head and reflect on these words:

There is a Light that lighteth every man.

Now bring the light down to the heart and into **your** heart. This spark of Light that you have brought forward and placed in your heart is warm and glowing. It is an indestructible Light and you have placed it in your heart.

And now, beloved, visualize if you will this spark of Light increasing in diameter, like a balloon inflated, becoming larger and larger until it becomes a room of glorious, radiant white Light, and you are standing in the center of that room. You are standing in this pulsating brilliance of Light, the Light that lighteth every man.

We would have you now visualize your Self becoming as two persons. Step outside that room of radiant Light and look into it at Self, and you will see that you have never been so beautiful, so radiant, so vital and strong. Encompassed with the white Light you are pulsating and radiant with all the healing colors of the spectrum. Your consciousness has never before been so filled with love, with peace as in that Light that lighteth every man. And this is the Light, beloved of the Father, which you have created. Just feel yourself standing inside this radiant white Light, feel the glow and the warmth. Feel this Light that **you** have created.

Now, standing within this beautiful brilliance, look directly ahead and see an altar. Fashion it as you will, it is yours. It is your place of worship where you may commune with that Infinite Wisdom called God. Visualize yourself kneeling before this altar of your own making, declaring your love and faith; making your decree of health and divesting the Self of all doubts and thoughts of contradiction of the Holy Light. Here you will make your declaration of wisdom, of abundance, and the Light dispels ignorance and restriction. Kneeling here at your Altar of Love, you may ask what you will, in the Divine Presence. And the Master said: "Ask, ask and you shall receive. It shall be given unto you."

We will leave you in silence for a while so that you may ask what you will in peace. And as you ask for things important to your way of life, speak in quiet conversation as you would with a person dearly beloved, stating your heart's desire, the most reverent wishes, your material needs, recognizing the power and the strength of the Light of Christ. (*Here allow a period of silent communication, prayer and contemplation, and then in your own time and when you are ready, continue the meditation.*)

Kneeling in this brilliance of Light, its blessings pour forth, vast, unlimited and so beautiful. This is a sacred room in your consciousness. Here you may leave anything and everything that you do not want to live with in your life's expression – old hates, fears, corroding guilts – leave them all there before your Altar of Love, and when you return to this your inner sanctum, they will be gone, because the Light does not encompass, it does not entertain, it does not preserve negativity.

You have made a place deep within the Self, the Spirit – a place most holy, the Holy of Holies, where you may meet every need, where you may go for rejuvenation, for upliftment, from which comes interior guidance. This is the ultimate shrine of every religion. This is the instrumentation of your faith. This is the Light of God in the life of Man. This is your Temple of Healing for your life, the Temple of Peace for your heart and of Strength for your physical body.

Loved ones, having accomplished these things, with reverence and thanksgiving, allow this Light, this warm, vibrant, glowing Light, to slowly diminish to that spark it was when you placed it in your heart. It will not be extinguished, because you placed it there deep within the Inner Self, and there it will prevail. There it will remain, warm, glowing and always available.

It is not possible, beloved, that you may enter this Temple of Love and Light without being blessed by that healing Divine Presence, the Divine Fact of Life, for your Temple is of your own creation and your own will. You have placed your Altar of Love and there abides that Eternal Light. Your body has become the Tabernacle of the Living God.

So be it. The meditation is now ended.

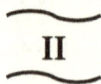

II

A MEDITATION FOR REBIRTH AND RENEWAL

With your mind transport yourself to your favorite beach at your favorite time of day on that beach. Hear the sound of the waves, note whether they are gentle ripples or big surfing waves. Feel the sand beneath your feet, whether it is soft and warm, or whether it is hard and cool because the sea has just washed over it. If it is day-time, feel the rays of the sun touching you. If it is evening, maybe you are in the glow of the moon. Perhaps there is a gentle breeze that caresses you.

Focus on everything on and around your beach.

Now start to walk along your beach. Maybe there are flying gulls that you stop to watch and listen to. Maybe there is a beautiful shell that you want to pick up, to touch and look at. Or perhaps there is a beautiful piece of driftwood that you can fashion into something lovely.

Focus on all that surrounds you on your beach, the sights that meet your eyes, the sounds that reach your ears, the feel of the beach beneath your feet.

As you walk long your beach, see in front of you a blazing fire in which the wood burns but is not consumed, and the flames are of such a pure gold they are almost white. Continue to walk towards that fire ... a big, big fire maybe eight or ten feet high ... and as you reach it, walk into the fire knowing it will not hurt you, but will purify you.

Stand within the flames of that purifying fire and be aware of the physical body dissolving away. There is no pain ... only joy and lightness. Now the physical body is gone completely, and you are pure spirit.

As pure spirit you seek to rise to the highest. Let your spirit take the form of an eagle. See the shining plumage, the majestic head, and feel the power of the great wings. Open those wings and fly to the sun. Soar ever upwards until your beach, your earth is an infinitesimal speck below you, and fly straight into the heart of the sun. Become one with that sun so that you are contributing to the rays sent by that sun to the earth, and put into those rays all that you wish for the earth and all who dwell on it. Know that as you give you too are receiving … you are being taught and given many truths. You are being filled with Divine Love and Compassion. Your eyes are opened and you See. Your ears are unstopped and you Hear. Listen to your Truth. Feel the Light filling your being. **Know** you are the Light as it is you.

(Here allow a period of silent contemplation and resume the meditation in your own time, when you are ready.)

Now, because in the world of Spirit there is no time as it is understood on earth, decide that you have spent much time in that world of Spirit and now wish to re-enter the physical world to learn more lessons there and to give to others what you have received in the School of the Sun. For your return let your Spirit take the form of a phoenix, a firebird, the symbol of rebirth, the bird that rises from its own ashes incarnation after incarnation. From your great height, with the measureless sight of the Spirit, look down on the beach where you left your former body. See that its ashes are still there, and fly down to them. As you take a position beside those ashes, breathe over them the Breath of Life and create a form, a body to house your Spirit.

Create this body as you would have it be, in full beauty and perfection. Create it so that it can be your channel to manifest to others the beauty you wish to manifest. Resume your human form, and step into that body you have created so that it is You … I AM that I AM.

Know with complete certainty that through this perfect body the Spirit can manifest all that you have ever been, all that you are and all that you are becoming. Know that there is no separation in Divine Mind, and that your Spirit, in whatever body it dwells, is One with the Father at all times and in every place.

Go in Peace. The meditation is now ended.

The next two meditations relate specifically to the Chakras, the seven centers of spiritual energy within the human body. These centers are located at the base of the spine, the spleen, the solar plexus, the heart, the throat, the brow (also known as the third eye) and the crown of the head.

Both of these meditations start with the attention focused on the base of the spine.

In the second of these two meditations, Gezala adapts the Prayer of St. Francis and applies it to the seven chakras. Each stanza should be repeated, aloud or silently, with the attention focused on the appropriate chakra, as listed.

III

A MEDITATION ON CREATIVE POWER

We would ask you now to put your attention on the chakra at the base of your spine, and visualize this center as a beautiful deep red rose in perfect bloom. Be aware of the color, the velvety perfection of the petals, the glorious perfume of this rose.

Now, keeping the image of the perfect rose in your mind, move your attention up the spine to the spleen, and see this chakra as a perfect orange poppy. See the translucent sheen of the petals, the perfect formation of the flower, the clarity of the color.

Now raise your attention to the solar plexus, and visualize this center as a yellow gladiola, its perfect sun-colored blooms gathered together at the top of a clear green stem.

As you continue to gather your perfect bouquet, move your attention to the heart chakra, and visualize this center as an exquisite pale green orchid, the color vibrant and clear.

Lift your attention to the throat chakra, and see it as a blue iris, its iridescent petals the symbol of the Three in One.

Now put your attention on the chakra at the center of the brow, the third eye, and visualize there an indigo tulip, perfectly shaped, the color pulsating with radiance.

Once again, raise your attention and focus on the chakra at the crown of the head and see it as a violet anemone, one of the lilies of the field.

Now gather together all these perfect blossoms ... the red rose, the orange poppy, the yellow gladiola, the pale green orchid, the blue iris, the indigo tulip and the violet anemone ... and surround this bouquet with three perfect white lilies, and know that your whole being is now a garden of perfect sweet-smelling flowers.

Now in the heart of that garden, in the heart of your being, at the heart chakra, plant the seed of Christ Consciousness, water it with the Light of Pure Spirit, and cause this seed to grow. Watch the seed grow and spread until it becomes a perfect golden rose at the throat chakra, the symbol of the Divine Creative Power in manifestation, and from this golden throat chakra, speak these words:

> I AM a source of endless Love,
> centered in the Light of Love Divine.

> I seek this source in you that in humility
> we may together build a point of Love Divine
> and send it forth, that all who recognize its

> Light may build anew.

The meditation is ended. Go in Peace and Joy, and let the beauty and fragrance of your garden bring Peace and Joy to all with whom you come in contact.

IV

A ST. FRANCIS MEDITATION

Introduction:	Lord, make me a channel of your Peace
Base of the Spine:	Where there is hatred let me sow love, and grant that I may not so much seek to be loved as to love.
Spleen:	Where there is doubt let me give faith, for it is in giving that we receive.
Solar Plexus:	Where there is despair let me bring hope, and grant that I may not so much seek to be consoled as to console.

Heart:	Where there is sadness let me sow joy, and grant that I may not so much seek to be understood as to understand.
Throat:	Where there is injury let me offer pardon, for it is in pardoning that we are pardoned.
Brow (Third Eye):	Where there is darkness let me bring Light, for it is in dying that we are born to Eternal Life.
Crown:	Lord, **I AM** a channel of your Peace.

Amen

V

A MEDITATION PRAYER

Make me a pure channel for Thy Power. Use me as an instrument of Thy Healing. Unto Thee I commend and give my hands, my mind, my Spirit. Use me according to Thy Will.

In the Name of the Master Jesus,

Amen

VI

THE THREE-FOLD FLAME MEDITATION

1. *The Violet Flame, which cleanses and transmutes*

Before using this Flame, call on the Law of Forgiveness.

"Beloved Magic I AM Presence, I call on the Law of Forgiveness for myself and all Mankind for all mistakes, misqualified energy, human consciousness and for straying from the Light.

Magic I AM Presence, blaze through and around me the transmuting Violet Flame, thy sacred fire. Purify and transmute now all impure desires, hard feelings, wrong concepts, imperfect etheric records, causes, diseases, effects and memories, known or hidden. Keep this Flame sustained and all-powerfully active. Replace all by pure substance, power of accomplishment and the Divine Plan fulfilled.

Beloved Lord Guatama, Archangel Michael, Mary and Ascended Master Jesus, charge into this Violet Flame your purifying dissolving power of Divine Love in its most powerful, dynamic activity."

See the Violet Flame coming from your I AM Presence, starting from below your feet and flaming upwards. (This is the only time the flame works upwards; normally it would start at the crown chakra). If you concentrate on it enough you can feel it starting at your feet. Just relax and concentrate on the Flame, and you will feel its movement. Allow it to envelop your whole body. Let the Flame soar over your head, and relax in it. This is also a form of discipline for the mind. Keep your mind on the Flame. Think about what it is doing; enjoy it.

"My Magic I AM Presence, charge me now with perfect health, joy, happiness, illumination, love, wisdom, power, abundant supply, with Ascended Jesus Christ Consciousness."

At this time ask for whatever you may require.

Pillar of Light

Feel this Light like a tube surrounding you. See it about three feet beyond your body. See the edges crystallize, and see the tube open at the bottom and the top. Like a switch, you can turn it on and intensify it and feel the blue-white Light and become one with it, feeling yourself as Spirit.

"Beloved Magic I AM Presence, intensify your protective pillar of pure substance and light in, through and around me, charged with your invincible protection, all-powerful and impenetrable, which keeps me absolutely insulated to everything not of the Light, and keep it sustained. Make and keep me ever sensitive to You and Your protection, and immune to all imperfect vibratory rates."

2. *The Pink Flame of Love*

Put your attention on your heart. Move the heart to the center of your chest and watch the Pink Flame flow out of it, and at the top of your heart see the Christ Light. Move your heart up your throat and to the top of your head and leave it there, but allow the Pink Flame of Love and the Christ Light to proceed on up to your I AM Presence, the Pink Flame on the outside and the Christ Light on the inside. You are now in the presence of your I AM.

Your Christ Light knows what you need at this time. Settle back and let your Christ Light and your I AM Presence take charge. Concentrate on the Pink Flame of Love; know that whatever you need for your unfoldment, to help you on your way, will be given to you at this time.

Bring the Flame of the Light down, joining your heart again. Feel your heart coming through your head and back down. Let it rest at your chest for just a minute and then let it go back where it belongs. One day, when our hearts will be completely purified and One with the Master, the right place for your heart will be in the middle of your chest.

3. The Blue Flame

"Beloved Lord Guatama, surround my protective Pillar of Light with your circle of Blue Flame and give me whatever added protection is required. I thank you."

See the Blue Flame about three or four inches around your Pillar of Light, circling it, giving the Light added protection.

Now, during the day, whenever you sense or feel (and it is good to even use it beforehand) something is not right, it just takes slight thought to move back into your Light and remember this is where you are, and that the Blue Flame is around your Light, keeping all discord away from you.

You can call on your I AM Presence at any moment of the day; speak to it as you speak with your Father, and you will feel it answering you with the Flame. It will blaze across your chest and you will know it is always there, giving you the assurance that we all need … that we do walk in Love.

(As stated on Page 10 of "Gezala's Teachings, this is a very ancient meditation, probably from India. It appears here as a translation in modern English, which nonetheless retains the essence and substance of the ancient original.)

Book II

Gezala's Words of Love And Faith

Gezala's Words of Love And Faith

Gezala's main theme in this, his second "book", is the power of Love and Faith, through whatever structure that Love and Faith are expressed. To the Father all Mankind are His Children, all One with no separations of any kind.

It is Gezala's hope and mine that these words of his will inspire you toward the goal of Universal Brotherhood and the eradication of hate and dissension, that the Prince of Peace may come to all Mankind and fill the Father's Creation with True Love, True Wisdom and True Peace.

Gezala's communications come after my daily meditations, at times of his own choosing, which I only know about when the spiritual writing starts. He knows that I am always at his service, which is the Father's service, and am eager to be his channel when he calls.

In the meantime, enjoy and learn from the words herein, and let the Light of the Father fill you. His Love and Blessings are with you always.

I

Unto God the Father be praise and thanksgiving that He has given us Life and Love, and the Will to serve.

How can we serve? By doing His Will, by having Love one for another. By never doubting Him and His Love. By seeking to understand the lessons in the things of our daily life. By helping His Children in any and every way we can. By remembering always that He is the Presence Within each and every one of us, and that we and all Creation are One with Him. There is no separation unless **we** choose to separate ourselves from Him. Even then, He is always there waiting in Love for us to remember who and what we are.

Go forth in the Love and Wisdom of God, serve Him and His Creation in Love, in Peace and Compassion.

II

There is no action a true Child of God can commit that will separate that Child from the Love of God. As we walk in the Light, as we are the Light we are One with the Living God. His Will is our Will, His Power is our Power and His Love is our Love. All that He is we are, and of His Endless Kingdom we are the Heirs. We walk in the Light as He is in and of the Light. Come before Him with praise and gladness. Sing unto Him a joyful song. Devote yourselves to the expression of His Will. All is His. In Him there are no dualities. He and He alone is Omniscient, Omnipotent and Omnipresent. Let none tell you otherwise. Do His Will and All will be added unto you.

Blessed are ye who hear and obey His Voice. Be not afraid. He is with you always and will never leave you. Broadcast to the nations His all-empowering Love. Be thou He as He is thee.

III

Why do men turn from the Father? He is Love; He Loves all His Children and wishes to give them that Love. But they turn to Mammon in their greed and their search for glory. What glory can they find that is like unto the Glory the Father can give them? O blind ones, open your eyes to see the Glory of the Father; open your ears to hear the Glory that fills His Creation and open your hearts to understand all that it means to be a Child of the Father.

What peace and joy do your material gains bring you? You are left empty because you are always seeking for more – more recognition or fame, more possessions – and what does the possession of more bring you? What but fear. Fear that these things will be taken from you; fear that their material value will lessen; fear that another will rise higher than you.

What do you gain by turning to the gifts of the Father? Peace, Joy, Happiness and the knowledge that no-one and nothing can ever take the Father's gifts from you. His Love is eternal and only you can stop its flow to you. The Father will never leave you. His Love is eternal and only you can cause you to leave the Father.

Change the dross of material possessions for the Glory of the Father's gifts and all will be well with you forever.

Selah, Shalom, Love

IV

What is the core of my being? None other than Love as expressed by the Father's Presence within me, signifying that He and I are One, and that we are One with all Creation.

Who shall stand against the Father? St. Michael and his Sword of Truth cannot help but prevail. The dark forces are seeking every way they can use to blot out the Light, but the Light shall overcome, dispersing the darkness and making every corner of Creation bright with the Light of Lights.

To bring this about all the Father's Children – the Children of Light – must join the Heavenly Host that is protecting those who cannot protect themselves, who do not yet know or accept the Light. Prayer, Meditation and Healing Love must be joined with that of the Heavenly Host and sent forth against the curtains of darkness. Love must and shall prevail and the Earth will move into the fourth level of being. It shall come to pass, as the Prophet predicted, that a New Jerusalem shall be built. It will be the Shining City on the Hill, drawing and lifting all unto itself and unto the Christed Life. All will be Light and Peace and the Brotherhood of Christed Love shall fill all Creation. There will be no more wars, no more hate, greed or envy, and the Father's Divine Plan shall be fulfilled in accordance with His Word.

So shall it be

V

All men must come unto the Throne of God. It is their destiny and their reward. For all those who love the Creator the Realms of Light await. The road may at times seem dark and drear, but ahead of the Pilgrim is Light and Gladness, Peace and Joy.

How does Man proceed to the Realms of Light? By loving the Lord God with all his heart, with all his mind and with all his soul. By loving his neighbor as himself, by having love one for another.

The forces of the dark are fighting a desperate battle against the Light, but fear not, for the Light shall prevail. The Children of Light – you, my beloved ones - must put forth Power and Light to join with the Hosts of Heaven to weaken these dark forces. You must send forth Love to them to turn their hearts to the Light. Bless them, for they know not what they do, but by sending your Love and Blessings to them, you will enable them to learn and to see the Light. Let your heart rejoice that you are the Beloved of the Father, that He dwells within you at all times. His Strength is yours; His Wisdom is yours and His Love fills you to overflowing. Therefore, go forth in His Name and fight the good fight.

Selah, Shalom, Amen

VI

I have seen the Glory of the Father. I have felt the Love of the Father and know He is always with me. How then can I fear anything?

His Armor is upon me and His Protection encompasses me. I stand ready to set forth His Will. I have put on the full Armor of God and have taken my place with St. Michael and the Hosts of Heaven. Light is shining on the Earth and the Light of the Father is prevailing. Those who have lived in darkness have seen a great Light. Let the Light of Heaven banish darkness and fear, sin and ignorance. Let the Light of Brotherhood enter the hearts of men that each may love those they looked upon as enemies. All Creation is of the Father and we are all equal in His Sight. Love ye one another. Throw away your killing weapons and grasp hands as friends – equal Children of the Father – that Love and Fellowship may erase war and hate. If we are all His Children how can we hate and destroy each other? Let Peace and Love be your watchword. Grasp hands as brothers. Do not inflict pain and sorrow, but peace and joy. Come unto the Mountain of the Lord and sing songs of praise to Him, the Father of All.

Shalom, Shalom. Peace and Love to All.

Benedictus

VII

I know that my Redeemer liveth, for He has shown me the Glory of His Being. I will ascend unto the mountain top and meet Him there face to face. His Glory shines around me and fills me with His Love, His Wisdom and His Strength.

I will ascend to Him and He will lead me in the Paths of Peace and Love.

Let Love fill my being that I may obey His Word – have ye Love one for another. I am His Child and His Light fills me. I will go forth in that Love and Light to help all those I can, to raise the spirit of those I meet and, above all, share Love.

Let not a word or thought of hate or criticism exist in my being. I am a Child of His Love, and this is what I must share.

He will walk with me in His Radiance and its glow will encompass me. I am One with the Living God and with His Christ, all those who have borne His Banner through the Ages of Man. Their strength, their wisdom and their love is mine and this I must express.

Hallelujah, Christ is risen and I will walk with Him.

Amen, Amin, Amen

VIII

They said to me "Come unto the Mountain of the Lord. Feel His Light fill you – the Light that is the Salvation of the World. None but He can lead you. None but He can encompass the world in Light and awaken its soul. All you who are of the Light, come forth. Cast the darkness from you. Disperse the darkness by piercing it with the Light."

Who can stand against the Light of the Creator? The darkness cannot stand nor can they who worship the darkness, who follow the commands of darkness, who accept greed, tyranny, the hurt and destruction of their fellows, those who seek to enslave all in order to feed their greed, their desire for dark power.

The Lord of Hosts has spoken, and the day of the unclean draws to a close. A new dawn is breaking and the New Jerusalem will be built. There shall be no darkness, no wars, no killings. Peace shall fill the planet, and Love shall be its watchword. The hour of Love and Light is coming. Praise to the Creator. His is the Earth and the fullness thereof.

Peace, Love, Shalom, Salaam. Love to all those who walk from the darkness, who repent of their errors and accept the Light.

Amen

IX

There is no end to the Father's Love nor to His Wisdom. In the quietude feel His Love and Wisdom fill you, and know there is no need of fear between you. You are One and therefore understanding comes silently. There can be no misunderstanding between you – you are One. He is your Loving Father. All He has is yours. Why then can you fear anything? Fear is the major inhibitor to growth, development and understanding. Did not the Nazarene say Perfect Love casteth out fear? And is not God's Love Perfect? Let this Perfect Love fill you. Make it your own, and you can then have nothing to fear.

Let the Holy Silence fill and encompass you. In the Silence the Still Small Voice will speak – again, not with words, but with understanding. Be thou whole and still. Jesus stilled the raging waters. Let not your life be drowned by the raging waters, but still all aspects of that life through the same Love and Power of the Father as filled the Nazarene. It is yours to command and use in the Name of the Father. You are His Child, you are One with Him. Ask and He will give you all Loving Power to do His Will and His Work.

Unto you is given all Wisdom, all Love, all Blessing. Seek it in the Holy Silence, and you shall Know.

In the name of Him from whom you came, all Blessings, all Love, all Peace. Amen, Shalom, Alleluia. God is All.

X

I have seen the face of the Most High, and its glory cannot be shown through others. His Glory lights the world and gives comfort unto Mankind. He is the Light of Lights, whose harmony and glory are directed to Mankind that they may enter into that Glory and be One with Him. He seeks to draw all to Him that they may know peace, love and wisdom eternal and never-ending – His Peace, His Love, His Wisdom, unlike anything we know on earth.

Lift up your hearts to Him, O Man, and great shall be your reward. His Love will encompass you and give you Peace beyond comprehension. His Wisdom shall show you Truths and Principles beyond your worldly knowledge, in which you will rejoice. Only in His Presence can these things be known. Accept, therefore, that He is the Presence who dwells within us all, and only awaits our invitation and acknowledgement to open all wonders to each one of us.

He is our Father, our Elder Brother, the fire of the Holy Spirit, and awaits our return to His Loving Arms.

XI

Love is the greatest power in Creation. Love will overcome all that we call evil. But remember that each Child of the Father must walk their own path. They must find their own way out of darkness into the Light. Each must do it in their own time, for only the Father knows their past, knows what Karma they must pay, and He will lead them, even if they do not acknowledge

Him. The day will come when the Light shall burst forth upon them and make them whole. Their way is not your way and your way is not theirs, but at the Father's Will their way will take them Home, as will yours.

The Nazarene told us "In My Father's House are many mansions. If it were not so I would have told you." Many mansions? Surely this describes the different forms of worship and philosophy before us. Who but the Omnipotent, Omniscient and Omnipresent God could have created the different forms of religion that are practiced in the Earth? Surely such a wise God would have known that the different peoples, the different cultures of His Creation would have different ways of understanding Him? What does it matter whether He is called God, Jehovah or Allah? It is His Being that is important and His teachings. What a pity that those who call themselves Christian are responsible for the spread of so much hatred. Our Father is a God of Love, it is Love that those who call themselves His Children should be spreading.

Again, the Nazarene said "Love your enemies". This is the path we should be taking to remind those who are still in darkness that they too are His Children, our brothers and sisters.

Let not your hearts be filled with the hate and violence that separate you from the Father, but rather filled with His Love.

Why do you think there is a greater power than God that can overcome His Creation? Everything in the Earth was and is created by Him, and there is nothing He did not create. The trials and tribulations we face are to bring us back to Him as we shed our lack of understanding, to remind us that He is our Loving Father with whom we are One, that He is the Loving Presence within each and every one of us. Therefore, my brothers and sisters, hear again the Galilean and obey Him – "Have ye Love one for another".

Shalom

~

XII

The Lord has spoken, and His Word is that Love must go forth. Love is the engine that will bring His Children together. His great commandments were "Thou must love the Lord thy God with all your mind and with all your heart and with all your soul" and "Love your neighbor as yourself".

Every Child of God is our neighbor. Every Child of God is the manifestation of the Father. How can we claim to love the Father if we do not love His Children in every corner of this Earth?

What does it matter what name we give the Father? He is still Omnipotent, Omniscient and Omnipresent. If I call only on "God", Allah and Jehovah will hear my prayer. He is One as we all are One. He does not acknowledge or accept labels. He knows only that all and everything that inhabits His Creation Earth are His Children whom He loves. If we wish to do our Father's Will, then we too must love all and everything in life, without exception.

Come before Him with rejoicing in total and complete surrender to His Will, in full and complete Love and great will be your reward, for this Earth will be a Heaven and all Creation will be blessed.

Amen, Shalom, Hallelujah. God is with us now and always. Blessed be His Name.

XIII

Come unto the Courts of the Father, and He shall feed you with the Bread of Life. His Love shall surround and support you. His Hand shall lead you on the path Home. Fear not to approach Him, for He is all Love, all Forgiveness and will let you dwell in the Realms of Light. Joyous shall you be, for where the Father is all is Light and Love, Peace and Harmony. He and you are One – the I AM of you is the I AM of Him. None can separate you from Him but yourself. His arms are always open in welcome. Fear not, for He awaits you in Love. His Courts are the Home of Homes. There is no pain, sadness or travail in His Courts. This is where you belong and where your new journey will begin unto everlasting.

XIV

Hear ye the Word of the Lord. Unto them that seek the Way shall open; unto them that ask the answer shall be given, and unto them that follow the Way of the Lord the Kingdom shall be given.

Has it not been said that the Father is with us even unto the consummation of the world? How then can it not be that we shall know the Way; how can it not be that we shall know all Wisdom and Truth as we receive the answers to our questions? We are the Father's Children. How can such a Father give His Children anything that is not true and wise? We are here to make this planet sacred, therefore have we been given the true tools of the Father. Let us then go forth and sow the seeds, tend them and reap the harvest of a world that is truly the Father's. Let our seeds all fall on the good earth, that they may grow in abundance and feed all the Father's Children with Truth, with Wisdom, with Light and Love, that the Second Coming – the Coming of the Spirit of Brotherhood – may indeed manifest through our work.

Go forth in His Name, His Wisdom, His Love and His Light. The Time has come.

Amen, Amen, Alleluia

XV

How can I express my love for the Father? By feeding His Sheep as He leads me to do. His is the One and Only Supreme Will to which I surrender. He will lead me and give me Peace. He will show me my Way Home. His Strength, His Presence within me will enable me to do His Will and fulfill the tasks He sets before me. His Wisdom will open all Truths to me, and His Love will sustain me through all. Without Him I am no-thing, can do no-thing. With Him I AM all in all and can do all He gives me to do; can face and conquer all the obstacles in my path; can grow to my full potential and arrive at last Home, where His Arms will enfold me and show me my Heaven.

Father, I AM yours, therefore you are with me always. Let your Voice be mine, your Thoughts mine and your Actions mine from this day forth even unto evermore.

I AM His and He is mine now and always. Great is the Lord of Hosts. Great is His Love and His Peace.

Alleluia, Alleluia. Peace be yours.

XVI

Now is the hour for the Son of Man to return to the Earth. Not in a body, but as a Spirit of Peace, Love and Brotherhood. No man can bring these things to the Earth, but the Spirit of God sends forth all these things. It is the time for the Children of God – Christian, Jew, Muslim, Hindu, Buddhist, all – to recognize that they are One, One with each other and, above all, One with the Supreme Being of the Universe.

What matters a name, a label. God, Jehovah, Allah, Buddha – all are One, the only Creator who made Heaven and Earth; the Creator who sent Angels of Light to the Earth to learn to love one another and to love Him. He is Supreme and He is the Father of all, even of those who do not as yet acknowledge Him. But His Patience is everlasting and eternal, and He will wait in Love until all Creation recognizes Him and responds to His Love and calls Him Father. Let no man mistake his destiny. However long it takes, each and every one of us will come to know the Light as it shines on our path Home, where we will be received with Love and rejoicing. Come before Him with love and thanksgiving, and He will return it to you a thousand-thousandfold.

Know ye are His Children and He the Eternal Light. Therefore take your way Home to Him. He has many mansions wherein ye may dwell and be with Him forever. God is eternal, ever-present, ever-wise and it is His Pleasure to give you the Kingdom. Praise to the Almighty now and forever. Alleluia, Alleluia, Alleluia. Shalom, Shalom in Love.

XVII

The Earth is the Lord's and the fullness thereof. He has created beauty for our dwelling place, and we have abused that beauty. How can Man expect to return to his real abode if he cannot treat his current dwelling place – His gift from the Father – with loving respect and thankfulness for the gift.

The Father filled the Earth with trees and flowers, seas and oceans, mountains and fertile plains, all of which are One with Him and with each other. In their Oneness they provided Mankind with every need. Beauty to uplift the spirit, food to nourish the body, animals to give us pleasure and for us to work with to preserve the planet. And yet greed and envy have caused us to forget these things are of the Father's Kingdom, and we have used them only for our own gratification and to increase our material wants. Where is the Love for all the Father's Creation? Where is the Love we are told to have one for another? Where is the love for our neighbor as for ourselves?

We are destroying God's Creation with fighting and wars, with pollution and destruction. But the Father has not withdrawn His Love from His Creation. To those who seek the spiritual path and walk it in Love He holds out His Hands to draw them Home. And the Earth too will be lifted into a higher dimension – the Fourth Dimension and then the Fifth – where it will live in restored beauty and peace, and the Father's awakened Children shall walk there in Love, in Peace, in Oneness and Understanding.

It is not too late, my brothers and sisters, for you to make this transition. Look to the Light of Lights, take it into your being and see it dwell there, casting out all darkness, hate and greed. Indeed, have ye love one for another and all else shall be added unto you. It is your Father's Pleasure to give you the Kingdom. He asks only that you accept it in Love and Honor, and treasure all that is given unto you.

Blessed be – the Father is with you now and unto everlasting. Be thou faithful unto Him.

Peace and Love be upon you. Salaam, Shalom, Amen

XVIII

Peace be unto you and unto your Spirit. The Father's Love shines forth upon His Children, bringing them Peace, Love and Wisdom. There is no end to the gifts of the Kingdom the Father wishes to share with His Children, but they turn away filled with anger, with hatred, with greed and with envy. They do not see that it is this that bars them from all that the Father has in store for them.

"Have ye love one for another." "Bless those who despitefully use you." The words of the Galilean still stand strong and steady. Why do men ignore or dismiss them?

There is so much goodness and joy awaiting all in life, if they would but open their eyes and see and unstop their ears and hear.

Was it not told you? Have you not heard? God is Love. He wants His Children to put aside all things that tend to separate them from Him. He will never leave any one of His Children. It is they that turn from Him.

Let your hearts be open to Him and His Words, to Him and His Love, that joy may fill your lives and you may find Peace and Rest in Him.

Now is the time for you and your Father to once again talk with each other, to know each other and to work together to bring all Creation into a new dimension of Peace and Love. Come let us work together that the Father's Divine Will may be made manifest and the time of true brotherhood dawn.

His Love, His Peace be yours now and always. Amen

XIX

The Father says "Come unto Me ye that are weary and heavy-laden, and I will give you rest. Come unto Me ye who are sad and grief-stricken, and I will wipe all tears from your eyes and give you joy. If I can do this for you, can you not see that it is My Pleasure to give you the Kingdom. All that I have is yours, for you are My Children, heirs of My Kingdom. My Love for you is vast and eternal, will never weary nor end. Look unto Me and set aside your cares, your woes, your worries. My Love gives you eternal Life, eternal Joy. All My Wisdom is open to you. You have known all that I know from the beginning, but you have chosen to obscure your memory. Let My Light shine on and through you, that your eternal memory may be clear. Now you shall see clearly and remember who you are and whence you came and why. You are My Children, made of my energy. You came from Me and shall return to Me. You came to Planet Earth to spiritualize the planet, to turn Man back to Me, that all My Children shall know

Me and My Love, shall follow the path set before them and shall walk that path Home to Me. There I await them, ready to take them in My Arms, to put the Robe of Love upon them and give them the Crown of Achievement, that we may all rejoice in the New Jerusalem, the new City of Light upon a Hill.

Come unto Me, My Sons, My Daughters, that we may know Perfection together. In Love and Blessing I salute you."

Shalom, Peace, Light, Love – Amen

XX

Let not your hearts be troubled. You know the Father is the Presence within each of you. Why then should you be afraid, why should you experience concern?

It is the Father's Pleasure to give you the Kingdom. All He has is yours. Why then should you fear your needs will not be met? Why then should you fear any danger? Why then should you fear the Father will abandon you? You are His for all eternity. He will never leave you nor forsake you. Remember His Arms are open to receive you. His Heart is full of Love for you – full to overflowing. Come unto Him in Joy, rejoicing that He awaits you. Give unto Him all your love, all your thoughts, all your actions, and your life will overflow with happiness and Light. Now is the time, for the day of change is coming, and His Children must be prepared. The Light of the World will encase the earth and lift it into a higher dimension where all will be Peace and Light and Love.

He said "Have ye love one for another", whether so-called Christian, Jew, Hindu, Muslim, Buddhist, Shintoist or any of the sects of separation Man has set up. You are all One in the Spirit, One in His Love. He knows no separation, but sees all Mankind as His Children. Come together as the family He created. Restore the Oneness of the day of Creation and be at Peace. This is His Word. Hear it and obey. Bless you in His Name, now and always. So mote it be. Amen

XXI

Not with the blare of trumpets comes the King of Kings. On silent feet He stands before the heart's door and knocks. When the heart is opened, silently He enters to dwell therein. And when the open heart becomes His Abode, the world is filled with His Light and in the still small voice He speaks His Wisdom and fills the world with His Love.

Sleepers awake! Do you not hear His knock? He waits, filled with Love for you. He waits at your door. Open to Him now. Know the fullness of Life His Presence brings. You and He are One, now unto the consummation of the world. Welcome Him and it will be His Pleasure to give you the Kingdom. All that He has is yours, if only you will answer His knock. Peace and Love will be yours, for if He dwells within you what harm or evil can come nigh you? He is with you. His Hand is upon you. You are surrounded by His Love, protected by His Light and upheld and sustained by His Wisdom.

You are His, He is yours. All Peace be unto you.

Shalom, Shalom, Shalom

XXII

How beautiful is the Father's Creation. How beautiful is the Peace of the Father. Now is the time to listen to the Silence, for out of the Silence comes the Voice of God. His Wisdom is all around you. His Love fills your being. His Strength is yours for the asking. Listen to the Silence. How it thunders with His Voice. He speaks to each and every one of us and gives us His Peace. There is nothing you need that He will not give you. Ask and ye shall receive, but the Wisdom of the Father may decide the wisest time of giving. Be not dismayed if there seems to be no answer when you ask. The Father knows the best time for you to receive. Remember a thousand years is like a day in His Sight, so to Him there is no delay – only a right time. Wait patiently upon the Lord and your need will be answered. But also remember that want and need are not the same. Look carefully at what you ask for. Make sure it is a need, not an empty want. Selfish desire will never be satisfied by the Father, but every need will be yours at the right time.

Beloved, know you are loved, now and always.

Amen

XXIII

The Word of the Lord is come upon the land. Hear Him, ye people. Now is the time to hear. He speaks in Love to all – to Christian, Jew, Muslim, Hindu, Buddhist, Shintoist. Whatever you call yourself, you are His. He has set His Seal upon the Earth, and the Earth responds. The time is at hand for the Earth and its peoples to lift up their hearts to Him and to move closer to Him. This earthly dimension is changing, and we and our planet are moving into a higher dimension. Woe unto them that have not heard, have not changed their thoughts to Love and Compassion, who still look on others of His Children as their enemy. Know you not that we are One - One with each other, One with Him and the multitudes of Heaven. Beware, for if you maintain this hate and separation, you will not be lifted up, for you will not be able to live in the new dimension.

The Day is breaking and you are still in the darkness of night. Awaken before it is too late. His Love is endless and eternal. He holds out His Hands to you, but if you turn from Him, He cannot help you. Hear His Call before it is too late. In Him there is no division, no separation. Every being – man, woman, child, animal, flower and plant of the field – are His and He calls all to Him. Hear Him now and answer – Lord, I come. Come hand in hand with those you have called your enemy. Bring your enemy in Love to Him and glorious will be the rejoicing in Heaven.

Let your watchword be always Love. Look to see who you can help, who has a need that you can answer. Look to those who are seeking but have not yet found as you have. Help all who come to you seeking, and you will lay up treasure for yourself in Heaven.

His Loving Hand is upon you. Turn to Him and give Him Love and Praise. He does not seek worship. He asks only that ye have love one for another, as He Loves you.

Now is the time. Come quickly to Him and great shall be your reward.

Alleluia, Alleluia. The Father is with us now and always.

Hail to Emmanuel – God with us

Amen

XXIV

Unto us the Light is given, and it shall drive away the darkness. Was it not said "Those that dwell in darkness have seen a great Light"? Indeed it is here for us to see if we will only look. And this Light will show us the way Home if we will but follow it.

What does the Light bring us? What does it show us? It brings us the Love of God the Father, which is unto everlasting. It shows us how that Love surrounds and fills us, if we will but look into it. Love and Light upon our path; Love and Light leading us to the place of everlasting Love and Peace.

Let the Light lead and guide you. It will wash away all your sorrows and lead you to Love and Life. It will cleanse you of all that is not of the Light. Your "sins" will be washed away and you will stand purified in the Light of the Father.

Be not afraid. He will not turn you away. He awaits you with loving arms open to embrace you. He is a loving parent who seeks only your good. Come unto Him and be at Peace. Know how much you are loved and rejoice in that loving. Come unto Him now and for all eternity. Hear His Word and come. You are His and He is yours. Love, Life and Peace await you.

Bless you now and always.

Amen

XXV

How do you know you have chosen the road for you? Is the way ahead dark, or does Light shine around it – are there shadows amidst the Light?

If the Light shines in golden glory on the road you have chosen, you are walking toward the Father. If the road is dark, you have taken a wrong turn, missed a path that was meant for you, and must look back over your choices and see what changes you must make. If there are shadows amidst the Light, you have started on the right road, but have brought with you some baggage that needs reassessment and probably needs to be left behind. A heavy burden will delay your journey, but if you come unto the Father and lay that burden on Him, He will give you release and peace, and the Light will shine brightly on your path as you journey Home.

Come unto Him in peace and love and His Arms will enfold you and welcome you Home. You are precious in His Sight and it is His Pleasure to give you the Kingdom. Why tarry you on the path? A myriad treasures await you, a Life lived in the Light of the Father. Make haste and come Home. He waits and will be with you through all eternity. You are His and He is yours.

Come Home, come Home. Bless you. We love you and bless you in the Light, you who are Children of the Light.

Blessing and Love be upon you now and always. Amen

XXVI

How shall the many be fed? By the seeds sown by the few. Did not the Galilean have a special circle who sowed the seeds and spread the Word of God? The seeds must be sown for the gleaners to come. The Bread must be prepared for the hungry to gather at the table. Seek not to spread My Word to the non-seekers. They are not your responsibility. The Father knows them, and in Love He will gather them to Him in the time appointed. Now it is time to work with the already enlightened that they may spread the Light, and those in darkness shall be awakened. The Word cannot be spread by those in darkness. It must be spread by those who are called. Do not be impatient, My Children. All will happen as the Father has decreed. Let the Word go forth through those who already understand it, that their understanding may create greater understanding. There is no need for haste – the time is moving as the Father decrees and only then.

Let you hearts be filled with Light and Love and heed the Father's Word. He is with you always and knows the needs of men. He will not fail you. Only you can fail Him by not heeding the Word. Let those who have opened their ears Hear. Let those who have opened their eyes See. Let those who have opened their hearts Understand. Now go forth and spread the Word in the way the Father has decreed.

Our blessing be upon you. Our love fill and protect you, now and always. Shalom

XXVII

I know that my Redeemer, my Father in Heaven, liveth. He is from everlasting unto everlasting. He is the Alpha and the Omega. He is the All-in-All. Without Him there is only no-thingness.

With Him there is All Creation. All that He has made is mine because I AM His Child. He will never leave me nor forsake me. He will forgive all my errors and welcome me with open arms. His love is boundless and forever. Let all Mankind rejoice in Him and give Him thanks and love.

Without Love we are no-thing and only through Love can we grow into the realization of who and what we are. Love has called us to serve and Love gives us the strength to serve. Put aside all thoughts of hate, of envy, of jealousy. We are One in the Spirit, and if we feel hate or envy or jealousy we are hating ourselves, envying ourselves, are jealous of ourselves, and this cannot be in a Child of the Father.

Gather at the Father's Table and share His Bread, His Love, His Light.

All that He has is yours. Accept it in love and joy, and give thanks that He Is.

Thank you, Father.

Amen

XXVIII

"To you who have answered my call I say Welcome. Welcome to My Love, to My Light, to My Wisdom, to My Strength. Now you know that I AM with you always. Now you know that the words you speak are My Words, the actions you perform are My Actions, the eyes with which you see are My Eyes and the heart that beats within you is filled with My Love. I AM you and you are Me and we are One in the Being. There is no separation between you and

I. As I Think, you Think; as I Love, you Love, and that Love must start with yourself, for if you do not love and cherish yourself, how can you love and cherish your brothers and sisters of the Spirit? All is One, so if there is any part of that Spirit that you do not love, then your love is not of the Spirit. Let this be a watchword unto you – have ye love one for another; love your neighbor as yourself. Do not separate yourself from any part of My Kingdom, for separation is not of the Spirit. Love is the Word, Love is the Action and Love is the Light. My Light must fill your being and be spread by you and all I have called. Go forth in Love, My Child, and send the Light to those who yet dwell in darkness. Love is Light and Light is Love, one and the same as you, I and all My Creation are One.

Be thou Me as I AM thee, for ever and ever, through all Eternity.

Amen"

XXIX

There is a river that all must cross. It is the river that leads to Paradise. What is Paradise? It is where the Father dwells and takes unto Himself all His Children. It is the river in which Certainty dwells and which all must pass through to rid themselves of doubt and fear. The river will cleanse and clear all who cross it. It will wash away doubts and fears and drown them in its sacred waters, and the renewed Child shall rejoice in its certain knowledge of the Oneness with the Eternal Father. Who would not rejoice in this Certainty? Who would not be glad of this Freedom? Who would not want to live in Paradise?

Therefore, Child, look at your doubts and fears, and see them for what they are – fetters that keep you from the Father. If you trust the Father, if you know the Father is Love, how can anything harm or destroy you? Fear and doubt have no power once you acknowledge your Oneness with the Father and His Love. The Will and Love of the Father is all that there is, and you are a manifestation of that Will and Love here and now. How then can you fear? How then can you doubt? Take courage and wade into the river and wash away these two impostors, and the Father and the Angelic Host will rejoice to gather you into their Fold.

Blessed be, now and forever.

Amen

XXX

Joy be unto you now and always. The joy of knowing the Father loves you. The joy of knowing that the Father, you and all Creation are One.

He has sent His Angels to guard, guide and protect you as you take your path Homewards. He will never leave you lonely and unprotected. How can you not feel joy in all that you do, as you do it unto Him?

Let your heart be filled with His Light, His Love and His Joy. You have nothing to fear, for you are His. He is always with you, knowing your every thought, your every desire, your every action. His guidance leads you and shows you the Way, the Way Home where you will live with Him, where you will know nothing but Joy and Love.

Take His Yoke upon you – it is light and no burden, but the guiding shafts that will make your journey easier.

The Way is filled with Joy, with Light and Love. Take it in Peace that passes all understanding, the Peace of the Father.

Travel in Peace toward Peace and know nothing but Peace and Love.

Blessed be.

Amen

XXXI

"My Voice and yours are One. Speak and write what I give to you. My Words shall be heard and treasured by those who understand. Each of My Children takes the journey in their own way. What is for one is not for another at this time. Each will come to the Truth in the appointed time, when they are ready to accept and understand. Do you ask a three-year old child to understand what an Einstein understood as an adult? Each of you must travel through the Seven Ages, and none can omit the understanding of any stage, as he makes his way through these Ages. I have set my plan and the pattern thereof, and as each Child walks his Way, great will be the joy and glory thereof. I know My Own and am known by them, and they hear and obey My Voice.

Peace and glory and Life in abundance be unto each and every one of you. You are mine and are known of me, and great is My Love for you all.

Listen, listen, Children, to the Christ Spirit within each one of you. The time draws near – be ready. So mote it be. Amen"

XXXII

I know the Way of the Lord, and will walk in that Way. His Hand is in mine, leading me, guiding me, sustaining and upholding me. His Love and His Light fill and surround me. I know that I AM His Child, and I know the Way I must take to return Home, to His Abode, where I will dwell and work for evermore.

Hear the Voice of the Lord as He calls you Home. His Words are of Love and Peace. His Arms are open to welcome His Child Home. Come unto Him and know His Love. It is yours now and always, and who else can love you as He Loves? Praise Him and give thanks to Him now and always, for His Kingdom is yours and all He has is yours. He gives them in Love. Love Him as He loves you and you shall know the Peace that awaits you. Come unto Him and rejoice, and great shall be His rejoicing as He welcomes you Home.

Peace and Love be thine now and forever. Shalom

XXXIII

Love is the Crown of Crowns. Love is the greatest power in Creation. Love is the great teacher, the great healer. Love, as St. Paul said, has no vanity, no envy, no anger. Has not hate done enough harm in your planet? Ancient enemies will not speak with each other, even though to do so would end centuries of death, of pain, of want. A few words spoken in Love could end the world's suffering, and open the door to Paradise. Love your enemies, do good to them who spitefully misuse you. The Nazarene said these things, and He said "Have ye love one for another. Love your neighbor as yourself and, above all, Love the Lord thy God with all of your heart, with all of your mind and with all of your soul. And yet Man has turned these very words into a reason to hate and seek to destroy other of God's Children who look to Him in different ways, whether Islamic, Hindu, Buddhist or any other man-made creed. The Nazarene also said "In My Father's House are **many** mansions". These mansions bear the names Islam, Hindu, Buddhist, Baptist, Catholic, Methodist, Episcopal and every other label Man has chosen to put on God's Word. God does not differentiate, so why should you? Love is the true label of God's Teachings, and all these teachings are of God.

Put aside your hate, your contempt, your anger. Embrace your brothers and sisters who name themselves differently than you do yourselves. God has no interest in labels, only in the development of His Children. St. Paul said "There remain Faith, Hope and Love, these three, and the greatest of these is Love". At no time did he say Love was limited only to those who think and express themselves as you do. Love is for all, therefore let your Love shine forth without limitation. God does not know limitation, nor should you as His Child. His Love of you is limitless. Your Love of His entire Creation should be equally limitless.

Let Love shine forth in your every word, your every thought, your every action, that you may truly adorn the Crown of Crowns.

Amen

∼ XXXIV ∼

Nothing in the world belongs to Man. It is all the Father's and He spreads His Glories for our use. But we, like naughty children, have put little value on what He presents to us. We have misused and ill-treated all the precious things He gave us for our use and pleasure.

What a jewel was Planet Earth when it was first created. The beauties of sea and sky, of forest and wood, of plain and meadow, of the great oaks and frail aspens, the beasts of field and home, and we have desecrated them. We have felled the trees, polluted the waters of sea and stream. We have caused the denizens of the wood and ocean to become diseased and ugly. We have caused the destruction of glaciers and ice floes, which in turn is causing the elimination of the species that depend on them. How long, O Man, how long can this destruction and misuse be allowed to continue? The Father is watching and waiting. It is not too late. Turn back now, O Man, to the pristine innocence in which you and your planet were created. Recognize your Oneness with all – with the Animal Kingdom, with the flora and fauna of the planet, with your fellow humans – your brothers and sisters – throughout the planet. Let Love be your true emotion and extend that Love to all God's Creation, of which you are a divine part. The time is NOW, before we destroy what the Father has created for you and your brothers and sisters. Be not afraid. God does not punish His Children. They punish themselves through their loveless actions.

Return to living in Love and let that Love fill the planet, that it too may bloom afresh, and we may continue to enjoy the beauty that God set before us.

Shalom, Amen – It is good

XXXV

Look to the Light. It shines for all. It fills and renews the Spirit within. It cleanses the inner being. It strengthens the weak. It enlightens those in darkness. It fills the despairing with hope. It brings new knowledge and Truth to those seeking it. It fills every need and truly creates an enlightened Child of the Father.

The darkness cannot stand in the Light. The Light dismisses the power of darkness and renews a right spirit.

From whence cometh the Light? From whence could it come but from the Father? The Father **is** the Light and the Light **is** the Father. He sends its glory to all who seek Truth, to all who know they are indeed One with the Father. For those who have been and still are living in darkness the Light is come to deliver them from travail. Their hurts shall be cured, their distress shall be as though it never was, and their hearts shall return to the Father, who has always been with them. The Father never leaves His Children, even when they turn from Him. He waits patiently until the Light again awakens their hearts and they turn back to His Love.

Follow the Light. It shines on your path and will lead you safely Home. Its rays are for your guidance and help. It will lead you safely, in Love, to the arms of the waiting Father. His patience is endless and enduring. His Love is with you for ever.

Turn to the Light, O Children. Receive and accept His Love, that you may live in that Light and in His Love in His glorious Kingdom for ever.

The Light has come. Embrace it and Live.

Amen

XXXVI

There is but one power in the Universe, and that is the Power of Love – God's Love for His Creation, Man's love for his fellowman. Love conquers all. Love lifts up all to the greater heights. Love sustains all in Peace and Serenity.

What does hate do? It separates man from man, country from country, neighbor from neighbor and Man from the knowledge of God's Love. God's Love is always around His Children, but their hate one for another blunts their awareness of that Love.

Hear again the words of the Nazarene: "Have ye love one for another. Love thy neighbor as thyself".

Have we so little love for ourselves? Do we hate ourselves so deeply that all we can give to others is that hate?

Let not this darkness fill your being. Dissolve it with the Light that Love sends forth. God is that great Light – the Light that expresses the Love that can wipe away all tears, can lift all sorrow from our lives.

Let the Light shine forth from you. Let the Love shine forth from you that God's Kingdom may indeed be built on Earth and His Children come into full realization of their Oneness with the Father, with each other and with all Creation.

So mote it be

XXXVII

I have heard the Word of the Lord, and I will obey. What a promise to make. What a joy to have to meet such a commitment. There is no greater joy than working in Love with the Father, in knowing that He, the Angelic Host and all Creation are One.

Let not your hearts be troubled. The Hand of the Father is over us all. He has set His Archangels and Angels to hold us in His Love. They will never leave us. Their wisdom and strength, their love and understanding is there for each one of us when we ask for it.

There is the hub of Life. We must ask. "Ask and it shall be given unto you. Seek and ye shall find." But the first condition is "Knock and it shall be opened unto you." Open the door of your heart and the Living Christ will enter and dwell therein. And once you have invited Him in, He will never leave you. He will dwell with you as One, and together there is nothing you cannot achieve in Love.

Love is the cornerstone, the foundation of all. Life must be lived through Love. And this means your Love must be extended to all Creation – even those who abuse you, who despise you and look down on you. How little they know. If your motivation is Eternal Love nothing can separate you from the Love of the Father, and if you continue to send forth Love to those you call your enemies, that Love will change them so that they are no longer enemies, but your brothers and sisters in Christ.

Love, Light and Blessings - – send them forth into your Universe, and your Life will be gloriously changed. You will walk in Peace and Serenity, holding fast the Hand of the Father, and all Joy will be yours.

Love ye one another in the Name of the Father.

In His Name, Amen

XXXVIII

In God's Love will the Soul be resurrected.

In God's Light will the Spirit sing.

In God's Kingdom will the being become whole.

Lift up your hearts and know you dwell in God's Love.

Lift up your voice in thanksgiving for the Light that fills you.

Lift up your mind to receive the Wisdom that will make you truly and consciously One with the Father, and with the Son and with the Holy Spirit.

God is Spirit, and they who would be One with Him – who would remember that they are One with Him – must be so in Spirit and in Truth.

Know ye that God is Truth. Listen for His Truth and let its Wisdom fill you, body, mind, soul and Spirit.

Give unto Him your Love, your Truth. For is not His Truth your truth and your truth His Truth. You are and always have been One with Him and will be through all eternity, through all Creation.

Behold His Love for you and give thanks. His Love is unto everlasting and can never be lost. We may sometimes forget who and what we are. We may turn our back on Him, but He never forgets who we are and He never leaves nor forsakes us. Be ye therefore at Peace. Remember you are His Child. You are One with Him always and ever.

Hallelujah, Hallelujah, Hallelujah. God reigns and we are His.

XXXIX

Life – what is Life? It is the manifested expression of the Father, who is our God. He has sent you forth, given you Life, that you may show Him to His Children – those who know and those who do not know as yet.

Love is His expression of Being. Only through Love can the union of all His Children be consummated. Love is the Keystone – was it not set in the City of Brotherly Love? Yes, but how many have forgotten the expression of Brotherly Love. Hate, anger, distrust – these flourish in so many of My Children today, as do envy, jealousy, bitterness. O My Children cleanse yourselves of these dark things. Let the Light into your being. Let your thoughts be of the Light, so that the Light bears all you do, all you think, all you speak.

The Light of the World came to you, but you have forgotten Him. He seeks to re-enter your hearts that your Life may be Joy, that you may have Life more abundantly.

All that the Father has is yours, and it only awaits your acceptance of Love as the engine of Creation. Have ye love one for another. Yes, we have said this often before, but have you heard? Have your ears been open to hear the Voice of the Father? Have your eyes been open to see the beauty His Love has created, to see where Love is needed? Have your hearts been attuned to His Words, telling you how to Live, how to Love your neighbor as yourself? Look, listen, think. Let this be your watch-word: "I am awake. I hear the Voice of the Father, I see the Beauty of the Father and I think as the Father. The Father and I are One. What more can I need, as long as I give of the Father."

Now is the hour when the Father's Plan will be revealed and will be consummated. Are you ready to do His Will and follow Him?

Go forth in His Love, with His Strength and Wisdom, and all will be well.

Shalom, Amen. Peace now and for ever. God is with you.

God is One

Hallelujah, Hallelujah, Hallelujah. Selah

XL

Joy to the World. The Lord is King. His Light is upon His Children. The Light fills them, cleanses them and renews their Spirit. Give thanks to the Father for all His many gifts, and resolve to keep these gifts before you at all times.

The gifts are first His Love, the Love that must be sent out to all corners of the Planet Earth, that wars may cease and all the Father's Children live together in His Peace.

Secondly, He gives the Light – the Light that illumines the soul and makes all clear and clean. The Light that shines on and is Truth and Beauty – that makes of this Earth an image of what is before us in the Father's Heaven.

Thirdly, He gives us Himself, dwelling within us, that the Wisdom working in us may make all the darkness disappear, will make the hills low and the valleys even so we may safely walk the road that takes us Home.

And fourthly, He gives His Peace, the Peace that passes all understanding, that gives us comfort that Love may fill the Earth and rise to Heaven.

Hear me, my brothers and sisters. We and every living being, every living thing in our world are One. One with each other, One with the Angelic Host and, above all, One with the Father. His Arms are around you. His Voice is in your ear. His Beauty is before your eyes, and His Love is in your heart. Therefore, have ye love one for another, for as you love one another, you love yourself, and as you love and accept yourself, the Angels in Heaven, the Father, Son and Holy Spirit Love you. And this Love will permeate your Being and the whole Planet Earth.

His Love and Peace be with you now and always.

Amen, Shalom, Salaam

XLI

God the Father is Good. God the Father is Loving. Therefore, what have we to fear. His Goodness, His Loving protect us from all harm.

God the Father is Light and as His Light shines upon us it dispels the darkness, it cleans our body and our Being, and it opens our eyes that we may see. Let not your hearts be troubled. He is with you, His Son is with you and the Holy Spirit is your Comforter. Let your heart and your mind be joyful. Let the Peace beyond understanding fill you. Let the Love of the Father pour into you, that you in turn may pass it on to your neighbor. Wherever there is sorrow, wherever there is pain, despair or want, send forth the Love of the Father to that place so that new Life may spring up and darkness be driven away. Even in despair the knowledge that the sufferer has the Love of God can lighten the heavy load and open the understanding to the possibility of new avenues, new prospects that the darkness has hidden.

Go to the Light, My Child, and a new day will dawn and you will be lifted up out of the gutter of despair into the Glory of the Father. He waits for you with open arms, His Heart filled with Love that is for you.

Rise, shine, for a new day is upon you, and all is well.

Amen

XLII

Rise up, O Men of God, and take your place at the forefront of the Father's Army. The Day of Light is near and the forces of darkness face their defeat. Your place is in the Army of Light, that the Father's Will shall prevail, and the time of Peace, of Love come forth.

Who can withstand the Father? Certainly not darkness, when God's Children stand ready to go forth in His Name. The time of Love and Blessing is at hand. Will you stand back and say "This has nothing to do with me", or will you play your part as an aspect of the Father? Come, my brothers and sisters, and walk with me on the path to Paradise. What could be greater than a time of endless Love, of endless Blessings, endless Peace. A time when wars shall have ceased, a time when hate has been wiped away, a time spent in the glorious Presence of the Father, the Son and the Holy Spirit. It will be a time – a golden time – when we know without doubt that we are One with the Father, One with each other, One with all Creation. Not only will we talk with God and all His Angels, we will talk with the aspects of God who have taken on the forms of the Animal Kingdom. They too will have been lifted into the Higher Dimensions and will communicate their knowledge of Oneness with all.

The Father has promised this, and the Father's Word is true. But Man must do his part to bring about the New Jerusalem. Man must put aside his weapons that kill. Man must cease to hate and persecute those he thinks are different to himself. Man must recognize that all Mankind and all animals of every kind are aspects of the One. When Man hurts or abuses another Child of God he hurts himself and shuts himself in darkness.

Heed the Light, my brothers and sisters. Leave the darkness and walk in the Light of the Father. Come unto Him and rejoice in His Love and Blessings. Let His Wisdom fill you so that you know the greatest word of all is Love. Love the Lord your God – your Father – with all your mind, with all your heart and with all your soul. Love your neighbor – every one of the Father's Children – as yourself. Have ye Love one for another as the Father Loves you.

Peace and blessing be unto you now and through all eternity.

Look to the Light and rejoice therein.

Salaam, Salaam. Rejoice

XLIII

The Father is Wisdom, the Father is Strength, but above all the Father is Love – Love abundant and overflowing, Love eternal and never ceasing, Love all encompassing, Love without end. Let not your hearts be troubled. You know you and the Father are One. You know nothing can separate you from His Love. Be at peace. All God's Kingdom is yours. All that the Father has is yours. Therefore, seek ye first His Kingdom and all else shall be added unto you.

His Wisdom will guide you and His Strength uphold you as you make your journey Home.

You have a question, a doubt? Ask of His Wisdom and you will be answered.

You have a task, a commitment that you do not feel strong enough to complete? Ask of His Strength and you will be strong enough to move mountains.

You feel lonely and desolate? Ask of His Love and joy will flood your being and you will soar as the eagle.

Nothing can overcome or deter you if you accept His Wisdom, His Strength and His Love as your own. You are one of His Angels, a manifestation of His Presence, and He awaits your return Home, when you shall rejoice in your Divine Oneness with Him.

You are His and He is yours. Be ye, therefore, joyful and sing songs of praise to Him always, now and forever.

Love and blessings be upon you. All is Light and Love, and you are His Child of Light.

Alleluia, Alleluia, Amen

XLIV

The Nazarene said: "Suffer the little children to come unto me, for of such is the Kingdom of Heaven", but who are the little children? We all are those children, and to enter the Kingdom of Heaven we must become childlike in the Eyes of the Father.

How do we become childlike? By remembering who we are. By putting back on the innocence of a child. By thinking only in terms of Love. By acknowledging, without any doubt, that we are One with all Creation, with all the Father's Kingdom. By accepting and living that there is no separation in the Mind of God.

God is a loving Father, who holds out His Arms to His Children, bidding them put aside their worries, their hates, knowing instead that all their needs will be met, and sending forth loving thoughts to all, caring for the planet the Father created for them, and loving the Father with all of their mind, all of their heart, all of their soul and all of their Spirit.

Love never faileth, but sends forth its power to lighten and lift all who accept it. Have ye love one for another, and the Father's Love will fill the planet so that there will be no hate, no wars, no destruction that destroys lives.

Come unto Him and Love. Accept His Kingdom, the Kingdom that is all yours, and great will be the rejoicing in Heaven, and joyful will be your Life on this planet as you journey Home.

The Blessings of the Father and of the Son and of the Holy Spirit be upon you here, now and hereafter.

Amen

So mote it be

XLV

How shall Man serve the Father? By obeying His Commands to love his neighbor as himself, by having love one for another and by loving the Lord Thy God with all your mind, with all your heart and with all your soul.

There is no greater power than Love. Hate and evil cannot stand against it, if the Love is pure and filled with the virtue of the Lord. If your heart is pure the Love grown in that heart will bring forth peace and harmony when it is shared with your brothers and sisters.

Where there is Love hatred cannot grow. It will wither and die like the seed that falls on hard ground.

The Temple of the Lord – the body that Man occupies – will grow in beauty if it is filled with Love. Let Love be your anthem, your manner of living, the very essence of your Being. You are a manifestation of the God of Love. You are He in action, in every thought, word and deed. You are His Messenger, sent to carry His Message of Love. He gives you the strength and the wisdom to carry out this mission. Do not fail Him. Let your thoughts and deeds always rest in Him, and He will give you all your needs.

Now is the time for Love and Light. Let your Light so shine forth that it will illumine the hearts of Man and bring forth into the Earth the Eternal Love of the Father. Then will His Peace and Kingdom be established in this Earth Planet, and the New Jerusalem be built, the Shining City on the Hill of Wisdom, Truth and Love.

His Peace fill and guide you. Let your Spirit bathe in His Love, the Eternal Love He gives you each and every day.

Now is the hour. Be thou ready. Love, Love, Love now and always,

Amen

XLVI

I said "What shall I write?" And He said "Tell of the Joy of Oneness – Oneness with all Creation, Oneness with all your brothers and sisters, One with Him who is the One, the Creator, the Father of all. Remember Him in your going out and your coming in, in your joy and gladness. But in your Oneness put aside all sorrow, for He shall wipe away your tears and fill you with joy. In Him there is no sorrow. In Him is Life and Love and Light. Shine His Light on the darkness within you and eliminate all darkness and sorrow.

Come unto Him with a joyful song. Let your Anthem of Joy sing forth into all the world. Let it ring, loud and clear, across the galaxies, into the outermost reaches of the Universe. Sing, my brothers and sisters, a joyful noise unto the Lord of Lords, He who has made you, He who Loves you and will never leave nor forsake you.

His Door stands open for you. Enter, therefore, into His Kingdom and rejoice. You are His Child and He gathers you into His Arms and spreads His Kingdom before you. All that He has is yours, as endlessly as His Love for you. Now is the hour for you to come forth and claim your inheritance as His Child.

Come unto Him in Joy and drink in the Light of Lights. The Door is open, the Way is clear. Therefore, be ye glad and rejoice in Him with whom you are One, who made you and loves you for ever and ever.

I am he who is Gezala, and in the Father's Name I speak to all who will hear, to all who seek the Light, that they may honor and serve Him with whom we are One, whose Love is upon all His Children, now and forever.

Amen

Book III

The Way to
the Realms of Light

The Way to the Realms of Light

*I*n this third book his focus is on how we can reach the Realms of Light in the Father's Kingdom, but again the major element in the Way is Love, Love, Love — for our brothers and sisters, the animal and plant world and, of course, for ourselves, because we cannot Love others unless we Love ourselves.

If God's Children on Earth can learn to live in accordance with Gezala's teachings, what a Paradise we will live in. And we must learn this lesson if we are to rise into the fourth and fifth dimensions with Mother Earth as she makes her ascent into the Light.

You were created Children of Light. Become carriers of the Light so that all can ascend into the Realms of Light.

Love and Blessings to all my brothers and sisters on Earth, and may the Light of the Father fill your Being always.

I

I have sought the Father and He has comforted me. My tears He has wiped from my eyes and my heart. He has opened the door of Joy for me that I may walk in His Garden of Peace.

Why has the Father done this for me? To express His Love and to fit me to be His instrument of Love and Peace, that I may send forth His Love to those in need, and bring His Peace and Comfort to the troubled.

I had thought my voice was nothing until I knew that I spoke with His Voice. He will give me the words to speak, the words to write. He will give me the strength to open my arms and offer comfort to those who grieve. Without Him I could do no-thing, but with Him I AM All in All. I know now with certainty that He and I are One, that through Him I AM One with all His Creation, and therefore I can complete the commitments of service I have made.

We are One in the Spirit, and as one centuries ago said: "No man is an island. Send not to ask for whom the bell tolls; it tolls for thee.". Anything that happens to one of the Father's Children also impinges on every one of His Children. We are here to spread love and understanding, to help each other, to give to each other without thought of return.

"To him who has it shall be given, and from him who has not it shall be taken." What shall be given, what shall be taken? Nothing but the knowledge of the Spirit, the knowing of the way to express the Father, the knowledge that each of us is the Father in expression and in action.

Open your hearts, my brothers and sisters, and welcome the Christ to dwell within you, to guide and direct your thoughts, your words and your deeds. And as He dwells with you, you shall know that you are His as He is yours.

Give unto the Father all that you are, and He will bless you and increase your knowledge of Him and His works and your ability to express Him and His Love and Wisdom.

As it was in the beginning, is now and ever shall be. Amen

II

The Father giveth to His Children the Bread and the Wine of Everlasting Life. To those who believe and serve shall be given the fullness thereof.

The Word of the Father never faileth. It is Truth and stands forever. Hear Him, ye who sit in darkness, who hide your sins in the darkness. The Light has come that Man may have Life and have it more abundantly. Let the Light wash you thoroughly. Let yourselves be cleansed by the Light, that your ears may be unstopped and your eyes opened that you may Hear and See. The Light shall fill you with Life Everlasting, and ye shall stand before the Throne of the Father, that He may welcome you in His Love, that you may rejoice in His Love and Peace. All that He has is yours. Wash yourselves in the Light that you may stand before Him and receive from Him your Home in the Kingdom.

It has been said "Though your sins be as scarlet, they shall be washed in the Light and ye shall be clothed in raiment white as snow." How then can you love the darkness more than the Light?

Is not the world gloried by the rays of the sun? How much more then can that glory be when filled with the Light of the Son? He came to fill your being with His Light, and that Light still shines upon you, but you see it not. Feel the Light anoint your eyes that they may be opened fully, and you will See all that the Father has prepared for you. Enter then into His Kingdom that He may give you all He has for you, that you may know fully all the Love and Blessing He has awaiting you.

Look to the Light and all shall be yours, my children.

Alleluia, Alleluia, Alleluia, Amen

III

There is no Presence but the Father; there is no Power but the Father. The Love and Power of the Father is all that there is. How do we know this? We know it because each one of us is the manifestation, the expression of that Love and Power, if only we acknowledge it.

We could know the expression of that Love every minute of every day if we gave up hating those who are different from us, if we gave up despising those we consider less than us. How often we forget that we are all One, all the Father's Children. Therefore, if we are all One and hate or despise any, we are hating and despising ourselves.

Why would the Father create only a monochrome of expression?

Are there not many different types of trees, of flowers, of animals? Why then should Mankind be of only one expression? Are there not twelve notes of music arranged by different composers into different forms, different tunes? Why then should Mankind be manifested on only one note? Every Child of the Father is as dear to Him as all His Children, and their color, their culture, their form of expression of worship is as dear to Him as any other. Let your hatred cease and be replaced by Love. Let your disdain fade away and be replaced by total acceptance of each other, so that the Father's Love may be known throughout His Creation.

We are One in the Spirit, we are One in the Lord, we are One in Brotherhood. Let this be manifested in our love for and acceptance of all of the Father's expression. Have ye Love one for another. Let it come to pass that the Lion and the Lamb may lie down together in Peace and Love, now and forever.

Amen

IV

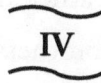

Now the hour has come. The Light shall disperse the darkness, and the Prince of Peace shall come to those who seek Him, and He shall dwell in the hearts of His People.

How can Man continue to express greed, scorn and hatred as the Light overcomes the dark? It cannot be, for as the Light stands as the Victor in the battle against darkness, Man's thoughts must become filled with Light and Love. If this is not so for those who still undertake a life of darkness, then they will not see or understand the New Jerusalem, they will not know the Prince of Peace who seeks to help them, and they must wait longer for this understanding to be awakened within them.

But Joy unto the Children of Light. Their Love and Light shall fill the Universe. They shall know Joy without end. And the Father will dwell in their midst for all eternity, as the Christ, the Prince of Love, dwells in their hearts.

Great shall be their abundance, everlasting shall be their home in the Realms of Light, and the Lion shall indeed lie down with the Lamb, and they shall eat straw together. There shall be no tears or sorrow in these great Realms, and none shall harm or kill another. The great Spirit of Brotherhood shall reign, and every Child shall care for His Brother and Sister. The Choirs of Praise shall sing their eternal hymns to the Father, and the Father shall bless all His Children of every race, of every color, of every culture and of every religious expression.

Love, Peace, Joy. What more can anyone ask than the Love of the Father, the Peace of the Father and the Father's Eternal Joy?

Welcome the Light, my brothers and sisters. Let it surround and fill you that you may send it forth to those who still dwell in darkness, so that they may indeed see a Great Light and be welcomed into the Father's Eternal Kingdom.

Hallelujah, the Light has come. Rejoice and be exceeding glad, and enter into your Kingdom.

Amen, Shalom, Salaam. Alleluia, Alleluia, Alleluia

V

The Universe and the fullness thereof is the Father's. He prepared it that His Children might dwell therein and know His Love; that they might grow in Grace and remember whence they came and why; that they might remember who they are and whence they are returning.

You have been sent forth to do His Will, that all might remember, might learn that their purpose is to spiritualize their earthly dwelling place, so that the Brotherhood of Man might come to full flower.

You have been told that the greatest weapon in your hand is Love – His Love that He has given you to share with all your brothers and sisters, that it may be spread throughout His Kingdom on earth.

Come, brothers and sisters – take up His Cause, use the weapon He has given you that all may be made manifest as He has set forth.

Now is the time for you to work as He has decreed. Go forth in His Name and sow the seeds of Love, for and with all.

As it was in the beginning, is now and ever shall be.

VI

What is Man that Thou art mindful of him?

Man is God in expression, the manifestation of the Divine on the earth plane. Man it is who can receive the Word of God and spread it amongst his fellow-beings. Man it is who can know the Love of God, the Wisdom of God and use these things to help his fellow-beings. Man it is who can know and experience with complete certainty that he and the Father and all Creation are One.

Why then would God not be mindful of Man, seeing that Man brings into physical earthly expression all that the Father wants His Children to know and experience?

Can ye not see? Can ye not know? The Father is Love and therefore Love must be the expression of His manifestations on earth. Let Love be your watchword. Let Love be your thoughts. Let Love be in all your actions. Let words of Love be the only words from your mouth. Ye are His Expression in all that you do, therefore be ye Him as He chooses to be you, to express through you and to manifest all His Kingdom by your deeds, your words, your thoughts.

Let your thoughts, your words, your actions be indeed His and His Kingdom will come, as it is written. Love Him and Love your brothers and sisters. Use His Wisdom and His Strength to meet your commitments to Him. Amen

VII

What am I to write? What does the Father want told? He speaks of His Love for His Children enduring for all time. But there is more. He asks why Man still will not hear His Words, still turns away from Him when He is knocking at the door, begging to be admitted, begging for His Children to understand that He and they are One. He does not mind what His Children call themselves, what their picture of Him is. He only cares that they turn to Him to know the Peace and Joy He can give them. What Peace and Joy are they finding today in the material world they have set up? Shiite kills Sunni, Muslim kills Christian, Hindu questions the right of Buddhist to live. This is not how God saw the Universe He created. He saw all living in harmony, loving one another, loving the animals that shared their world, each learning from the other. But Mankind has turned away from Him and will not heed His Voice, except in small numbers. Those who have seen the Light, those who have heard His Voice must take up the responsibility He has placed upon them, and go out into the world with His Words. Even a small number can work miracles. How many disciples did the Galilean have? Twelve. And yet what a miracle they wrought. His teachings still ring throughout the world, and if only Man would listen to them and obey them, what a world would result. Unfortunately, greedy men found a way to change the teachings so that they would have power over their fellows.

Jesus taught that there was no need for an advocate between God and any of His Children, but rather that each could talk to the Father in their own way. But greed set up a church system whereby the priests of whatever religion could demand tithes, could put their own interpretations on the teachings and thereby separate the Father and His Children. This is not the Father's Way. He said: "Come unto Me, ye who labor. Lay your burden upon Me and I will give thee rest. Take My Yoke upon you and learn of Me, for My Yoke is Light and My Burden is easy.". He did not say go to a priest, an iman or a guru, but told us to go to Him directly.

Therefore, my little ones, listen to His Voice. Come to Him with your burdens and He will take them from you. He asks only that you love Him, that you love your neighbor as yourself, that you care for and nurture the earthly kingdom that He gave you, and that you follow His Way and prepare yourself to join Him in the heavenly kingdom that He has prepared for you.

God is Spirit and like Him you too are Spirit. You and He are One in the Spirit, and together you can do all that He has given you to do. He has declared that the Prince of Peace is coming, is indeed waiting only for Man to fill his being with love instead of hatred. Can you not hear this Prince, the Christed One, knocking at the door of your heart, begging you to open to Him? Answer Him, O my dear ones, and ask Him to enter, to fill your being with His Light and Peace that the New Jerusalem may be built, that the end of war and hatred may be accomplished and that all may live in His Love and Peace through all eternity.

The Father gave His Children free will that they might choose their way of life, but many have forgotten who they are and whence they came and have turned their backs on the Father, thinking only of what they can gain for themselves – what wealth, what fame, what material possessions – and ignoring their brothers and sisters in need. The Father will not force His Children to follow His Way, but He longs to show them what abundant joys await them if they do. Look to the story of the Prodigal Son, dear hearts, and remember what joys awaited him when he made the decision to return to the Father's House. This too is your choice – darkness or Light. Be careful how you choose, beloved of the Father, that you may enjoy all the gifts of the Father's Love rather than a life of darkness. The Father will not make the choice for you; you must make it for yourself with a free will.

Blessed be the Father and the Son and the Holy Spirit now and always. Amen

VIII

What says the Father?

"Ye are My Children whom I Love. I open the wonders of Creation to your view. I hold you in My Arms, My Loving Arms. My Love is ever with you and for you. I offer you unbounded Joy through My Love. The vistas of the Realms of Light are open to you, and await your coming. Know you not that you can visit them each and every day by your own choice? What are the Keys of the Kingdom – why, only Love and Peace, Brotherhood and Peace. My Peace is everlasting and filled with Joy. Be thou My faithful Child and earth cannot tell nor understand the riches that await you.

Let your heart be free and open. Put aside any desire for material things. What need have you of earthly possessions, of earthly wealth or earthly fame? These are hollow and empty things. My Love, My Peace, My Joy are so much more, give you so much more, and are everlasting. Earthly fame is fleeting, earthly possessions can crumble and fade, earthly wealth can turn to dross and leave you poorer than ever. But My Love, My Peace, My Joy are everlasting and shall be unto you as a sweet perfume, as a glorious vision, as riches beyond earthly dreams. All that I have is yours. You are heirs of My Kingdom, which is unto everlasting. Come unto Me and Peace and Joy beyond earthly understanding shall be yours.

Let Brotherhood be your way of life, and the doors of My Kingdom shall be opened to you.

Let Love guide you in all that you do, and the riches of My Kingdom shall be yours unto all eternity.

Be thou Me in action, in thought, in word, and we shall always be as we are now, One in the Spirit.

Open your heart and let Me dwell therein and be your Inspiration and your Guide, now and always. I AM yours and you are Mine, and we are altogether in the knowing, One in the Spirit.

My Blessing be upon you now and for evermore.

Amen."

IX

Let the Voice of the Lord be heard in the land. Let the people hear and rejoice. His Love is for everlasting, and His Words speak of Love. Hear ye His Voice. Listen to His Words. Accept the Love that He has for you, with which He surrounds you each and every day. Great is His Love for His Children, and His Words teach Truth. Listen, listen, understand and be at Peace.

His Peace He gives you, but you accept it not. You war with each other for the treasures of the earth planet, treasures which have no value and which shall fade and be blown away as dust on the wind. But what the Father gives will not fade, will not be blown away, but shall be yours for all eternity.

Peace, Love, Wisdom, the Trinity of Everlasting Life. If you dwell in Peace you will hear the Still Small Voice of the Father, which will guide you over the straight and narrow path to your home in the Father's Kingdom. If you dwell in Love you dwell with Him always. Have ye love one for another. You are all His

Children, how then can you not Love one another. Live with His Wisdom, and all shall be known unto you. There is not anything He will not teach you through His Wisdom. All that the Father has is yours. All that the Father has is indeed yours. All the Father's Love is yours, all the Father's Wisdom is yours, all the Father's Peace is yours if you will but open your heart and your mind and your soul – your whole being – to Him.

Listen for His Voice as you work in His Peace, using His Wisdom and His Love, and your Life will be enriched beyond human understanding. It has been said "Lay not up treasures for yourself of the things of the earth", and this is a true saying. But lay up the treasures that the Father gives you and great indeed will be your wealth – all that the Father has.

Watch and be ready, my Brothers and Sisters, for the hour foretold is coming, when the earth shall be filled with the glory of God as the waters cover the seas.

He is yours as you are His. Watch for His Coming.

Amin, Amen, Salaam, Shalom. All Peace be yours. All Love be yours. All Wisdom be yours unto everlasting. Benedictus

X

Come, come unto the Garden of the Lord, where all is Beauty and Peace. The flowers give forth a radiance of sweet perfume that purifies all who are aware of it. The leaves of the trees gleam with the Light of Love, and therein dwell all manner of birds whose sweet songs fill the air with the glory of heavenly music. The Devas work at the Father's pleasure to keep all bright, lovely and peaceful, the flowers, the trees and every aspect of the Garden always at the peak of Beauty.

All who dwell therein know the Love and care of the Father, and send forth that Love to all Mankind that they may know and live by it. In this Garden none can hate or envy, but all know that they are One with the Father and all His Creation. Here brother walks with brother and sister works with sister, whether they were called Jew, Christian, Hindu, Muslim, Buddhist or any other creed labeled by Man. All know they are One in the Lord, One in the Spirit, now and for all time.

Is not this how the Father's Children should live – in Peace and in Love? In the Garden of the Lord **all** are His Children, He cares not whether male or female, and to this must we all come if we are to enter and dwell in the Garden. Know this and be ready. Remember, each of us, in our various incarnations, have been male, female, black, brown, white, red, yellow. How then can you despise or war with what you have been and will be again before you dwell forever in the Garden. Therefore, put aside your ill-will, your anger, your disdain, your envy. They are not the keys to the Garden. Those Keys are Love, Compassion and Peace, and only they can open the Gate.

Your Paradise awaits. Prepare yourselves that you may come Home in Joy.

Amen

XI

Whence cometh the Light? The Light comes from the Father, from God, for the Light is God and God is the Light. He shows

Himself to us through the Light, for to look upon Him directly is not possible for human eyes. His Glory is magnificent and radiant, and while Man still inhabits a human body, that Radiance is beyond his ability to see. But when the Children of the Father are ascended, when they themselves are bathed in that Light, the Face and the Glory of the Father will shine forth upon them in all its wondrous radiance.

Look to the Light, My Children, and prepare to stand before the Father as His Radiance surrounds and uplifts you. His Light is one with your light, and as you grow your light will become ever more radiant and you will be received into the Realms of Light, where dwells the Father, knowing and touching every part of His boundless kingdom.

He knows each and every one of His Children, and calls them by name. Hear His Voice calling you to Him. Know that His Love and Light await you as you grow. Know that as that Light and Love fill and surround you your life shall be sweeter and more joyous. Indeed, you shall know greater and greater joy as you accept that all the Father has is yours.

Let your being be open, here and now, to His Love, His Light, to all that He has in store for you. You shall know your life is eternal, as is His Love for you.

Light, Love, Joy – the gifts of the Father to His Children. They are yours now and forever in the Realms of Light, as the Light fills the Father's Creation.

Look to the Light. All is yours. Rejoice in His Love and be whole.

Amen

XII

How shall I express the Father? By pouring forth His Love. How shall I praise the Father? By feeding His sheep and His lambs. How shall I express my Oneness with the Father? By working in His Wisdom and His Love. It is for me to show His Love, His care for His Children. It is for me to work only in Love, to send forth Love, to bind the hurts of those who are wounded, to dry the tears of those bowed in sorrow, to give loving answers to those who are lost and confused. It is for me, as the Father tells me, to gather His sheep into the fold, that they may know peace, that they may come safely home into their haven.

I AM God in action and expression. My thoughts are the thoughts He gives me, my actions are as He directs, and my words are the words He wants spoken. Let my being be open to Him always and ever, for He is the Fount of my being. Without Him I am as nothing, but knowing our Oneness I AM all in all. Everything the Father has is mine and stands ready for all His Children. As His Child it is for me to awaken other of His Children that still sleep, that they may know this wonder and glory.

Open my being, Father, that at all times I may do Thy Deeds, speak Thy Thoughts, and send forth Thy Love to all you bring to me. Wash away the darkness in my being, that Thy Light may shine forth and lighten all you bring to me. I AM your Channel. Use me now and always.

You are the Light of the world. Let all men see and be amazed at the beauty of that Light, at the Glory of Your Love and the wondrous Peace that you give to all who call you Father.

In Your House there are many mansions, mansions to house all your Children of every faith that Man has established. Therefore, let us recognize that we are all One with You, that there is no division in the Kingdom of the Father, and that at the Father's Will we all will live together in Love and Unity – One with Him and with each other.

In Love, Wisdom, Peace and Faith.

So mote it be.

XIII

He said "Write", and I said "What shall I write?". And He answered tell the Children of Light that the Father has need of them. The Powers of Darkness still fight on, and though the Light must win this battle for the souls of Man, the Children of Light must stand against the darkness. The Father has called home many of the greatest of the Children of Light that they may stand with Michael and the Sword of Truth. The Light shines forth from the Father. It encompasses the Army of Light and is sent forth to the Earth and His Children who dwell there, so all may stand against the darkness that the Light may prevail.

Rise up, Children of the Light. Let your voices be heard as ye speak of Truth, the Truth of the Father. You have distorted the Truth by the way you have split into contending groups and sects. There is but One Truth, the Word of the Father. Therefore, put aside your differences and speak with One Voice. You and the Father and all creation are One, therefore your words should be giving forth One Truth.

I know not why you have separated. Always you were One, but in your desire to experience life as a human, you have allowed your Oneness to be shattered and separated. Return to your beginnings, Children of Light, and rebuild your Unity, your Oneness with the Father. He is One with you and all your brothers and sisters if you would but recognize and accept it. The Will, the Power and, above all, The Love of God is all that there is. You, I and all Mankind, each of us, is a manifestation of that Will, that Power and that Love.

The Peace of the Father passes human understanding, but we can build an earthly peace in the Name of the Father, that we might attain His Peace. Remember the prayer "Let Peace begin on Earth and let it begin with me". Begin to build peace that the Light may encompass all, and help us all to attain that Heavenly Peace. Now is the hour. My brothers and sisters, do your part in His Name.

So mote it be. Amen

XIV

Hosanna, Hosanna unto the God of Light and Love. He sent His Light into the world, but the men of darkness saw it not, although they felt its power and were afraid. The Light taught Man how to live abundantly, but the men of darkness corrupted His Words and His teaching, and deceived the people of earth on what he had taught.

Love **is** the fulfilling of the Law. Love is the path to Paradise. If ye have not love, ye are as empty vessels.

The men of darkness, in their corruption, did set up places of worship, but designed that the worship be of them and their perceptions. They sought power for themselves and taught not what God had said, but what they put forth as the words of the Father.

The Father has said that each and every one of His Children can come to Him directly, needing no intermediary between them and Him. Go into your quiet place my brother, my sister, and talk to the Father as you would any earthly friend. He will hear you and will answer you, and the words you hear will be His Words as He himself sends them forth. You will not receive His Wisdom as misconstrued by one seeking his own power, but exactly as the Father knows you need and want to hear. His Love and His Guidance are ever present, ever there for you to receive. You and He are One, and He dwells always within you. His Presence is ever with you. Call on Him and He will hear. Know Him as your friend and abide in His Love and Peace. No harm shall come nigh you, and you will know His Presence always.

Worry not. Let worry and concern leave you. You cannot lose His Love. His Patience is endless. He knows you will come fully to Him at the time that is right for you, and He will welcome you with open arms and all-encompassing Love.

Love, Light and Blessings be upon you, now and always. Amen

XV

What shall I say? What shall I do? Only that which the Father gives me to say and do. His is the voice that speaks, His the action that is performed. Without Him is nothing said or done. His is the Will that speaks and works through His earthly channels. Nothing is created that He does not create.

The Love, the Will and the Power of the Father is all that there is. I must be and am a manifestation of that Power, that Will and always that Love.

Love is the energy of the world as expressed by the Father. Therefore, Love must be the motivation of each and every one of the Father's Children. Let your heart be filled with that Love. Send forth that Love into every corner of creation. Where there is need, seek to supply it. Where there is hate, seek to turn it to Love. Where there is pain, seek to heal it. Wherever help can be given to any Child of the Father, let yours be the heart and hand that gives it.

Be thou the Father in thought, word and deed, so that you are a pure channel for His Will and Love, now and always. So may it be, so it is, as it was in the beginning, is now and ever shall be. Amen

XVI

Know you not the Love of the Father? Have you not heard of that Love? Did you not believe in that Love?

The Father loves each and every one of His Children and, like any parent, He sorrows for them when they are hurt, when they feel alone. He knows this is only because they have forgotten Him, moved away from Him or denied Him. But He is still there, His arms held out to them, His Being filled with Love for them, awaiting only their remembrance of Him, awaiting their return to Him, awaiting their acceptance of Him.

How can such a Love be denied or forgotten? The answer is that Man has turned to things of the Earth and forgotten his own spiritual origin. Man has found that he prefers to gather material things to himself, and call them wealth. How much more rich is the wealth of the Father. All that He has is for His Children. It is His pleasure to give them the Kingdom that they might have life more abundant, but Man in his darkness prefers the dross of materiality, and passes by the wealth of the True Spirit.

Turn back to the Father, my brothers, my sisters. Man and time cannot tell all the joys and wonders of the Father's Kingdom. There you can dwell in Peace, in Harmony, in Joy, loving one another and being loved. Great is the Kingdom and great are they that dwell therein. There is no hate, no envy, no anger, no unkindness. From out of the Father's Love come richness of life, peace beyond understanding and love that is eternal.

Leave the dross behind you, my brothers, my sisters. Accept the riches that are yours. Do not let the cock crow thrice on your denials, but shout aloud your acceptance of the Father, the teachings of the Son He sent and the comfort and understanding of the Comforter that is among us, the Holy Spirit – the Spirit of Truth.

There is an old saying, "Count your blessings". It is good advice, and, as you count them up, let your joy, your thankfulness to the Father swell within you and give thanks.

If you accept the Father, the Christ, as the Presence within you, all that the Father has will be yours, and great will be His Joy that you have accepted it.

His Love and Blessings be with you, now and always, as it was in the beginning, is now and ever shall be. Amen

XVII

How shall I tell the glories of the Father? Who can tell of Him as He is? But we look not to His Glory, but to His Love, His Wisdom, His Strength. We give thanks for His Patience as we strive to follow His Will, as He leads us Home to Him.

Know you not that He is always present with you? His Love pours forth upon you to give you Peace. His Hands seek to embrace you to give you His Eternal Love. His Wisdom is yours for the asking, to enlighten and awaken you. From this Trinity – His Love, His Strength, His Wisdom – unknowable Joy shall flood your being and His Light shall fill you and make all clear unto you.

Let not your heart be troubled. Your belief shall make you whole. The past is no longer yours to carry. Let all sorrow, all grief, all sins, all unknowingness fade from your being, and in their place fill yourself with the cleansed Beingness of Oneness with the Father. The past is gone, the future is yet to be. Live now in the present and do those things given you to do. You have made a contract with the Father to be His channel, His instrument, that His Love, His Wisdom may be known to Man. Now is the time to fulfill that contract. Now is the time that the New Jerusalem <u>must</u> be built, and in that building you must play your part. The foundation stones have been laid. Now must each faithful Child of the Father come forth to build the walls with stones of Truth, to set the City aglow with the Light of Brotherhood and everlasting Love, to set the music of the spheres ringing through its streets. So may we all live in Peace and Love and glorify His Name.

Give thanks, my brothers and sisters, that you are the Father's instruments in the here and now, to bring about this Age of Brotherhood and Love. Give thanks that His Light has shone upon you, and is guiding you Home.

Blessed be His Name, now and forever. Hallelujah, Immanuel is among us and the Glory begins.

Amen, Amin, Amen

XVIII

Have you met the Christ? Is He known to you? He knows you. He it is who watches over you, guides you, leads you and protects you.

If you know Him and know He dwells within you and in all the Father's Children, your life path is open to you, the Way is plain and the road clear. He it is that sets the guideposts on your Way. He it is who makes clear to you how you must travel, what lessons will face you, what decisions are ahead of you.

Let Him in to your heart. Open the door on which He has knocked and ask Him to enter and dwell therein. Listen to His Words, accept His Love and Wisdom, and all will be well with you, no harm will come nigh you. You are His as He is yours. He is the Good Shepherd who knows you by name, and will protect you in all your goings out and comings in. He will not leave you desolate or alone, but offers you His Presence, His Comfort and His Love.

If you will be faithful unto Him, He will be faithful unto you now and forever.

Welcome Him, embrace Him unto everlasting. Amen

XIX

Make straight in the desert a highway for our God. Open a pathway for our Lord. Why say you that you know not the highway, know not the pathway? Live you only in the arid desert? The Word has been spoken often and again, the Word that straightens the highway and makes plain the pathway. You have heard it, but have you received it? The Word is Love – Love for the Lord your God, Love for your neighbor, Love for yourself. You are the Child of God, the channel and the instrument of God. How can you do the Father's work if you do not Love yourself as that Child, as that channel, that instrument, for the Love you express is the Love of God.

God loves you. Will you turn aside from that Love by casting yourself in the dust?

Rise up, O Child of God. Know you are loved and are worthy of that Love. Then, when you Love yourself, you can send forth that Love into the Universe, to every man, woman and child, to every creature and every flower, every plant, everything in God's Creation. Call all your brother, your sister, your friend. All are One. There is no separation in Divine Mind, therefore there should be no separation in any part of God's Creation.

Let your Love so shine forth that Men will call you blessed. Know that you are One with the Father, that He is yours as you are His. Know He dwells within you, is part of you eternally. Know He calls you to do His Work, that the darkness may be driven from the Earth, that the Earth and all its peoples may be bathed in the Divine Light, cleansed of all sin and darkness, and born to newness of Life in the Light. Know Life as abundant as the Man of Galilee promised. Know Eternal Life, dwelling in and with the Father, in His Love, in His Light and with His Blessings.

May the Holy Breath fill you now and forever with the Blessing of the Father-God, as it was in the beginning, is now and evermore shall be, world without end.

Amen, Amin, Amen

XX

Who Am I? I AM a Child of God. Who are you? You too are His Child. You are my brother, my sister. We are all One in Him, who is the Father of All.

Were you not told "Have ye love one for another – Love your neighbor as yourself"? How then can you not love your brother, your sister. Each of us has a mission on Planet Earth, a mission we were born to undertake, a mission we made a commitment with God to complete.

What is our mission? Our missions may be expressed in many different ways, but the basic concept is to spread the Love of the Father, the Light of the Father. We are here to work together to bring about God's glorious Kingdom on earth. We are here to learn to live in God's Peace one with another. We are here to help each brother and sister realize that they are each God in action, fulfilling His Will and bringing about the New Jerusalem.

How can we do this? By listening to the still small voice within and obeying what it tells us to do. By surrendering all that we are – body, emotions, mind and soul – here and hereafter to the Will of God, knowing that without Him we can do no-thing, but with Him there is not anything we cannot do.

Welcome Him, the Christed One, to dwell within you. Open your heart to Him, and you can change the world. Know He is One with you and you can do miracles. Did not the Man of Galilee say "Marvel not at the things that I do, for greater things than this shall you do"? And so we can and will if we do as He directs us.

Let Light fill you, let Love become all that you are, and you shall bring to pass all that the Father desires of you. Go forth in His Name, and you shall accomplish great things.

Peace be unto you. The Love of the Father fill and sustain you now and always for all eternity. Amen

XXI

Now is the hour when the Father speaks to His Children. He brings to them remembrance of His Love. He teaches them His Wisdom and He fills them with His Strength. To each He brings a special message, for each Child is different, is taking a different path and has different needs. All these things the Father knows and He addresses each and every one of them according to need.

Let your hearts, your minds, your eyes, your ears be open to Him. Listen in the silence and you shall receive all that you need, all that will help you to draw ever nearer to the Father.

And how is this teaching to be manifested? By loving your neighbor as yourself; by remembering that he who dwelleth in Love dwelleth in God.

The greatest need in the world today is Love, and yet brother fights with brother, sects denounce sects and backs are turned on the suffering millions. We have been sent to this planet to spiritualize it, but we look only to our own needs, our own greed, and forget to help our brothers and sisters who may speak a different language, have a different look and worship the Father in a different way. These are only outer differences. Each person, male or female, dwelling on our planet, is a Child of the Father. To each the Father gives His Love, but it saddens Him to see and know that the emotions which have the greatest outpouring among His Children are hate, greed and personal satisfaction. If you do not care for your brothers and sisters, why should the Father continue to care for you? Why think you that only you are special, that only you know how to worship the Father, that only you know His true name? "In my Father's House are **many** mansions" said the Galilean. His Father, who is also ours, has many mansions because He created many types and cultures of Man, and He gives to each what that culture needs. Because we are His Children it is up to us to act as He would have us do – to accept all His Creation and Love each and every being therein.

So let your Love shine forth. Leave your hate, your greed, your envy in the darkness where it belongs, and step into the Light of Love. Let your Light shine before men that they may recognize the Child of God you truly are and may take you as their shining example. So shall the Father be glorified, and His Kingdom indeed come into being on Earth.

So mote it be. Amen

XXII

What shall I write this day? What words has the Father given me to say? I AM Gezala, a member of the Father's Magic Circle, but what do I mean by "magic"? I do not mean clever conjuring tricks, unillumined clever actions that mislead. I mean the Glory of the Father, the Light, the sacred illumination of the Father, the Light of Light that He sends forth to His Children, whether on the Planet Earth or anywhere else in His Creation.

You are the carriers of that Light. To you He has given the power to send it forth into every corner of darkness, to dispel that darkness and lead your brothers and sisters into the Light. His Command is clear:

You are Spirit as He is Spirit.

You are Light as He is Light.

You send forth Love as He is Love.

To all His Children He says: "He that dwelleth in Love dwelleth in God. If you walk in the Light as He **is** the Light, you have fellowship one with another". And that fellowship shall change the Planet Earth. It shall call forth Love and Light and full knowledge of the Father and all He wants for His Universe and for His Children. All that He has is yours, and He has it stored for you at Home.

Rise up and heed His Call. Let us seek that brotherhood, that unity that is ours from the beginning, now and forevermore. Turn your faces to the Light and see Him as He holds out to you His Love, His Wisdom and His Strength. Once you know and accept that you and He are One, that His Presence dwells eternally within you, there is nothing you cannot achieve. You can sing His praises with the Angel Choirs. You can write of His Glory with the great masters of words. You can build within you a Citadel of Light that all may know Him.

Come unto Him. Receive His Light, His Wisdom, that you may partake of His Glory through all eternity. He will not fail you nor forsake you. He is there for you always if you will come unto Him in Love and Light.

Why wait? Come now, that your life may be more abundant and you may know Love beyond all human understanding.

So let it be.

XXIII

Come unto the Father rejoicing. He is your strength, the host of your Being. His Grace is your only need, your only supply. Feel His Love fill your being, strengthening and enlightening you. And how shall this Grace fill your life, change your life? By your answer to it.

It is not yours alone. It is given to you for sharing with your sisters and your brothers. It will never run dry. The more you give, the greater shall be your supply. Remember how the Galilean fed the multitude with five loaves and two small fish? In the same way shall the Father's Love and Wisdom multiply in you as you share it with His other Children. Only he who clutches his treasure to himself shall lose it. To him who has it shall be added; from him who has not it shall be taken. Why? Because he who does not share is not awakened to Divine Knowledge and Truth, is not aware that he and the Father and all Creation are One, but thinks only worldly possessions are his happiness. He holds dross instead of the pure gold of the Spirit of the Father, and unless he awakens and sees the Truth, only dross – which is nothing – can be added to his nothingness.

Welcome all the Father's Children into your heart. Give unto them of the wealth your Father has given you, and know you are blessed of the Father and that you stand among the angels before His Throne. To them that give unto others, much shall be given. They shall be numbered among the chosen, and shall rejoice in their Oneness with the Father. All that the Father has is theirs and yours, therefore you have much to share. His glorious Light shall fill and surround you and give you His Love and Peace for evermore.

Glory be to Him and to His Children for ever and ever. Amen. Hallelujah, Hallelujah. So mote it be. Amen

XXIV

Today I am beginning again, not from where I was, but from where I AM now. I have reached the end of a stage of my journey and am at the start of the next stage.

What has changed? What is before me? I have realized that while we are all One, at different times we need different aspects of that Oneness in our lives. As we grow, these different facets of the Oneness are presented to us as our next goal, our next step. The Oneness is a multi-faceted diamond, presenting different points from which to view our journey. The facets shine Light on new roads, new journeyings, new companions on the way. And so it is for all of us.

But let us remember we have not lost the former companions. Their spirit is still with us and always will be. The fact that previous companions no longer physically journey with us does not mean they are lost to us. It simply means their path takes them on a different road, which may be quicker or may be slower. Each of us has our own path to walk in our own time, and new companions can perhaps help us more, or we can help them more, as we walk that path.

This does not mean that those former companions who no longer walk with us are "better", "more advanced" or "brighter" than ourselves. Maybe they have a greater or lesser karmic debt to pay. Perhaps they had walked further along their path in an earlier incarnation. It matters not. We are all destined to arrive Home at the end of our journey, in the time that is right for us. The Father waits in love and patience for us all. When we arrive He will be there, His Love shining in glorious Light, the Robe and the Feast ready.

As we journey, it is our duty to help those we meet along the Way, to make sure they are aware of being fully in the Father's Love for all eternity. "Have ye love one for another", and your journeying will be filled with wondrous Peace, with the knowledge that all the Father has is yours, and great shall be your reward in His Kingdom.

Go, therefore, in Peace and Love, strong in the Strength He gives you, fully aware that His Wisdom is yours for the asking. Know at all times that he whose thought is stayed on the Father will experience Life eternally full and overflowing, filled with Love and Glory. So shall it be as it was in the beginning, is now and ever shall be.

Thanks to the Father and to the Son and to the Holy Spirit. Great is the Love with which we are blessed as we take our journey Home.

Shalom, Salaam, Amen, Amin

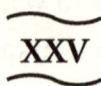

XXV

You ask "How shall I, with my human weaknesses, serve the Father? How shall I awaken my Divine Strength?"

By remembrance! By remembering who and what you are. How can you have forgotten, when the Father and His Archangels are around you eternally?

Remember to believe and say – "I AM One with Him and with them, therefore all that He is and all that they are is mine. Their Strength and mine are One, and is available to me when I call on it. His Lovingkindness and theirs is One with mine, and is always mine to express for the asking."

Remember to believe and say – "His Wisdom, theirs and mine are all One, and open to me when I call on it. All that the Father has, all the qualities of Michael, Gabriel, Raphael and Uriel are in me if I awaken them."

I, Gezala, have heard you say, "The Father calls me His Child whom He loves. And do I not love my Father in return? O but His Love is infinite, eternal. In my forgetfulness I have allowed mine to become only human. Forgive me Father and help me to awaken my Divinity. I call on Michael, Gabriel, Raphael and Uriel to use all they are to this same end, an end which is indeed a beginning." Well, my dear one, here is your answer.

Let the Light of a new day of loving expression dawn in you. The Age of Peace and Love is stirring within all of the Father's Children who hear His Voice. They will rejoice and give praise unto Him who holds before us all the True Pattern of our Being.

Unto Him forever be all glory and thanksgiving, as He restores and welcomes His Children Home to His loving arms.

You ask forgiveness, beloved. It is yours for the asking, through all eternity. Where there is great love, forgiveness is always available, and great indeed is the Father's Love for you and all His Children.

Now I say unto you, Glory Alleluia, Christ is come and His Loving Wisdom fills us all. Amen, Amin, Amen.

Glory be to God on high, and to the Earth Peace.

XXVI

I have known the Father from all eternity, and He has known and knows me. We are One. I am His tool, His channel that He uses to send His Love and His Wisdom to all His Children, even those who do not as yet hear or heed His Voice, those of His Children who feel lost – lost because they do not hear.

Listen, O Children of Man. He speaks to you in Love. He calls you to Him, to give you His Love. All His Kingdom is yours; all the Glory is yours, but you turn only to the shallowness of Caesar's world. Why seek you the sham worthless things, when He holds out to you untold glories, the real, the true, the priceless gold of His Kingdom?

Why run you after false gods of greed, empty wealth and worthless material things, when the True God holds out His Arms to embrace you with Love beyond human understanding, with the priceless treasures of His Love, His Wisdom, His Strength, His Grace? Know you not His Grace is your total supply? All that you need He holds for you, and waits only for you to turn to Him that He might give it to you, that you might have Life abundant and overflowing through all eternity.

Give unto Him your praise, your love, your obedience to His Law, and you shall see and experience Heaven in your life on earth. He is only a breath, a prayer away. While you heed Him not, He watches over you in Love, protecting you from the perils your ignorance and heedlessness bring into your orbit. His every wish is that you will turn to Him and accept His Love. But He will not force you. He has given you the free will to make your own choice whether to accept Him or not. The choice must be yours, but once you turn to Him, once you ask in truth for His Love, it will be yours without question.

O my beloved brothers and sisters, make the choice and knowingly become One with Him. Rejoice in the glories that will fill your being, and be glad unto Him, now and for evermore.

He is yours, you are His, together as One, in Peace and Love eternally.

Rejoice in the Lord, and be glad that he awaited you through all eternity. And so it is.

XXVII

In the Father's Strength is ability. In His Wisdom is Truth. In His Love is True Being. In His Grace is all supply.

They who receive these gifts and use them in the Father's service, shall know True Unity with Him. But they must be used in joy, without thought of glory, of renown or any reward. It has been said that it is in giving that we receive, and this is Truth indeed, for if we give in Love and know that Joy of giving, we have received abundantly. The Father has filled our cup full to overflowing in the full knowledge and understanding of His Love. What more can we need, what greater reward can we receive than that Love? From the Father's Love and Grace flow everything to give us a full life. As we receive from Him and give to those in need, we receive the Bread and Wine of eternal life. All that the Father has is ours, and He gives to us the abundance of eternal life. Now, in this hour, accept from Him the bread and meat that will ensure you never again hunger, the wine of life that will mean you will never thirst again. Your nakedness will be covered and your shelter will be assured.

Let this be the answer to your giving now and always. Know He is with you now and always, and that you can never be separated. Once you have taken His Hand, He will never leave you. Once you fill yourself with His Love and Light you can never know loneliness or darkness. In surrender to His Perfect Will and Love you rise to glorious Life and unbounden Joy.

Open your heart fully to Him that you may be filled with Love and Light unto evermore. Amen

XXVIII

"I have set your hand to write My Words. I have set your heart to carry My Love. I have set your mind to seek the Truth of My Words, of My Teaching. You are My Child, whom I love. You are My Channel whom I inspire to spread and teach My Words.

Let not your heart be troubled. You believe in Me and My Love. You believe in My Wisdom, and you accept My Strength. My Grace is always at your call. We are One in Love, in Creation, in your Being, in abundant Life.

Therefore, my beloved, go forth in the full armor of God. None can harm you, none can stop you but yourself, but if your belief outweighs your doubt, if your doubt has been washed away by your belief, then none can stand against you.

We are One as we have always been, and now and evermore shall be."

Thus speaks the God of Hosts, the Father of us all. Thus He arms His soldiers for the fight against the darkness. Thus He strengthens their arms and their minds, that they may know the forces of darkness cannot stand against them.

Go forth in Joy and Love. Spread the White Light of the Father to all His Children. It has been said "They who dwelt in darkness have seen a great Light". Be the bearers of that Light, ye who are the Children of Light, who are the Light of the World.

They who sit in darkness long for the Light. The darkness overwhelms them, but they know not how to call forth the Light. Let your mission be to carry the Light to them, to show them that the Light is theirs for the asking. Show them the Father only waits for them to ask in Love and all His Kingdom shall be theirs.

Go forth in Love and Joy, Children of the Light. Let your watchword be "The Father is with us. We and God are One."

Our Love and Blessings be upon you all, now and through all eternity.

Amen, Shalom. Peace be with you.

XXIX

The Lord of Hosts has spoken. He has given His Word to Man that Man might know and understand who and what he is; that Man might know there is no separation in Divine Mind, and that he and the Father and all God's creation are One.

How can man make divisions between himself and those of different races, different skin color, different cultural and worship formats? Does man not realize that he is condemning himself, cutting himself off from vital aspects of himself? Every man, woman, child in the Universe, every animal, every plant and flower are all One in the Father. Why then do we turn against our brothers and sisters, condemning them because they do not express themselves in the same tongue and method that we use?

"In My Father's House are many mansions" said the Galilean. Yes, I know I have referred to this before, but it seems that Man of Earth does not accept that the many mansions are there for each of the different aspects of the Father's Children. He has prepared many mansions because he has created many peoples, many peoples to express different aspects of His Being.

It cannot be that man thought God was so limited that He could only create one species. Does not man know that the Father is Omniscient, Omnipresent and Omnipotent? This being so, the Father can create, as He has, multitudinous peoples, worlds and universes – multitudinous yes, but all are One.

It is not fit that man should seek to harm and kill his brothers and sisters, but it **is** fit that he should express to them all the Love of the Father. The Galilean said to Peter: "Feed My Lambs, feed My Sheep". Now we know the lambs and sheep are all of the Father's Creation, our brothers and sisters, the animals given into our care, the plants and flowers, the fields and oceans all given to us to be cared for. Therefore, we should use all these things with Love, thus expressing our Love of the Father and giving thanks to Him for all these gifts.

And this is only the beginning. All of the Father's Perfect Kingdom is ours, and His Love for us and His Gifts to us are without limitation.

Let the Love and Light of the Father fill your Being. Let this Love and Light direct all your thoughts, all your works and all your acceptance of everyone of the Father's Children, and great will be the Love, the Wisdom, the Understanding that the Father pours forth upon you.

In His Name, In His Love, His Blessing be upon you now and always. Amen

XXX

Write, my child. Write of the Father's Love which knows no end, is eternal and enfolds each and every one of His Children.

There is no Man of Earth who is without the Father's Love, but sadly there are many who do not know it is always there for them.

How sad their empty lives must seem. But you, my child, and all the Children who do know, have life abundantly. Maybe their material needs are not always met; maybe their material possessions are small, but great is their Joy in the Father. Every one of my brothers and sisters who walk in the Light of the Father live joyously. They know that the Father's Grace supplies their every need, now and always.

What more can anyone need who knows the Father's Love, the Father's Grace? All that the Father has is theirs.

Come unto Him now and feel His Love, His Peace. "They will live in Perfect Peace, whose mind is stayed on Him". His Love will lift up His Children to the Mountaintop of Joy. He will fill their minds with Perfect Peace. There will be no confusion, no doubt, but only Perfect Love without fear, without hurt. "God will wipe all tears from their eyes." The radiance of His Light will shine round about them through all eternity.

Come unto the mountaintop and meet your Father face to face. Feel His Arms around you, supporting you every minute of every day. Feel His gentle Hand caressing you into good sleep at night, so that you rise restored into the Light of the new day, ready to do His Will, His Work in blessed service to Him.

Fear not, my brothers, my sisters. The Life Abundant is yours for the asking. Speak to Him. Tell Him your desires, how you seek to serve, and swift will be His response and great will be your comfort.

The Galilean said: "My burden is Light and my yoke is easy". Take up the burden of the Light that your service may be easy.

Blessings, Love and Peace unto you, Children of the Father. Blessed be. Amen

XXXI

In the renewal of Spirit is the Father's Love shown forth. In that Love is the Grace, the Wisdom and the Strength of the Father.

If we have Love, if we live in Love, if we share Love with all that is in life, we have the strength to do the Father's Will and to send forth the Father's Blessing to all that is in life.

Our Strength will never falter, and we will be filled with the Love and Grace to recognize the Christ Spirit in all we meet, whose pain, longing and desire we can help through the Power and Will of the Father.

You think you do not know how to help others? O dearly beloved, remember who and what you are. You are all Children of the Father, and if you accept Him and surrender to His Love and Will totally and completely, you will be One with Him, and He will give you the words to say, the actions to complete, that you will indeed heal and help the broken, the weary, the seekers and the needy Children of the Father. He will never fail you, for you are His Channel, His Instrument to send forth His Love to all His Children. He is with you always, and His Love, His Will, His Power flow through you, now and always, for all eternity. Your faith has made you whole and set you as a Light to show the way Home to the Father to those in need and in pain, who have forgotten Him and turned from Him. But through your words and actions they can be reminded of their true Beingness, and they too can be made whole again.

Give thanks, dearly beloved, that you can do the Father's Will, and that you can hear His Voice, and consciously know His Love. Sing praises and thanks to Him, and be exceeding glad that His Hand rests upon you, now and always.

God be thanked for every blessing. So mote it be. Amen

XXXII

In the Father's Hands are Love, Understanding, Mercy and everlasting Patience. He watches over His Children as they make their life's journeys, blessing them, forgiving them, and waiting for them to turn to Him.

He knows the trials they bring on themselves by forgetting Him, or even not knowing Him. He sends His Love to them every minute of every day of those lives, asking them to turn again to the Light, asking them to recognize and accept that they and He are One, to know and accept that all He has is theirs.

Children of the Father, turn to Him now, that He may give you all He has in store for you, that your life may be lit by His Light and His Love. Why do you tarry in the darkness when your life might be made glorious through His Light? The Light of Life will shine upon you and fill you with all the beauty of God's Perfect Kingdom. It is already yours if you will but turn to Him, accept Him as the Loving Father He is, and know with all your Being that you and He are One.

This planet on which you live is going through a major transition. Mother Earth has tired of the abuse that men have heaped upon her and has called on the Celestial Beings to help her cleanse herself. A glorious new restored Mother Earth is preparing herself for life in a new and greater dimension, where God's Children will live in Love and Harmony with all there is in life. But if you remain in darkness, turning your back on the Light, you will not be able to rise with her. Do you really wish to live in darkness, in hate and obscurity? As a Child of the Father, you were created a Being of Light. That Light is still flickering within you, and you can restore it to the Pure Flame of creation, burning brightly for you and all your brothers and sisters.

Let your Light so shine that your Life may be protected and perfected, that all may be drawn to you in Love and you may indeed lift up all your companions to the radiance of the Father.

Light, Love and Blessing – the fulfillment of the Father's Creation.

Love, Light and Blessing be upon you now and eternally.

In His Name, so mote it be.

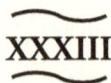

XXXIII

Let not your tongue speak judgment. There is only One who judges, and that is the Father. His judgment is benign and loving, to help His Children, not destroy or decry them.

You cannot judge your fellowman, because you do not know where he stands in his Being. You do not know what karmic debt he may be paying through his behavior in his current incarnation.

What do you know of the past incarnations of your brothers and sisters? What do you know of their need to "clean the slate"?

As Mother Earth ascends to her new dimension, those that inhabit her must be cleansed, with every karmic debt paid in full. The Mother's dwellers must be pure as driven snow, shining as the sun. They must live only in Love and Kindness, in the desire to help, not hinder, their brothers and sisters. The Apostle Paul said it centuries ago: "Only these three remain, Faith, Hope and Love, and the greatest of these is Love". The Galilean said it when He proclaimed two laws for Man to live by: "Thou must Love the Lord Thy God with all of thy mind, with all of thy heart and with all of thy soul" and "Thou must Love thy neighbor as thyself".

Speak not then in judgment of your neighbor, of any of your brothers and sisters. Bless them with your Love and grant them the strength to fully pay any karmic debt they may have.

And look to yourself, beloved. What debts must you clear? Have you been loving, kind, understanding? Or have you been envious of another's bounty? Have you been angry at what you saw as injustice committed by another? Do you know whether that "injustice" was or was not earned by an injustice the apparent victim committed in an earlier incarnation?

Love, Love, Love. This should be your banner. This should be your gift to all your brothers and sisters. Leave judgment to the Father now and always. He is a fair and true Judge who works only for the good of His Children. Do thou the same.

In His Name and Love, so mote it be.

XXXIV

How does man turn from the Father? By greed, by hate, by unkindness, by lack of mercy, by cowardice, by dwelling in the halls of malice.

How can man turn again to the Father? By the joy of sharing all he has, by sending forth thoughts of Love into the universe to his fellowman, by giving forth compassion, even in little acts of kindness, by treating all his fellowmen, even the so-called criminal, with mercy, by acts of bravery to save those in peril and, again, by putting aside malice and turning it to Love.

The Planet Earth is suffering from the lack of Love. Many of those who dwell there have thought only of increasing their own material possessions by plundering Mother Earth. Where are the Father's trees? Hidden under acres of cement, destroyed without thought for the consequences, to build and build and build again to cover the forests, the hamlets, the parks, the fields, whole areas that once were beautiful and life-giving, life-enhancing.

Dear Ones, this must stop.

The Father gave you a land of beauty in which to spend your earthly incarnations, but you have destroyed that beauty. This is **not** the path to the Realms of Light. This is the way to plunge the planet into the darkness forever. But Mother Earth is taking her own steps to prepare for the ascent into the next dimension, and only those who follow her lead will ascend with her; the rest will be plunged into eternal darkness.

O my beloved ones, look to the Light. The Light is Love and Light and Love are the way to eternal life in the Realms of Light.

You are all Children of the Father, the bearers of His Light. Let your hearts fill with His Light that you may be bearers of His Love to all your brothers and sisters, with whom you are One in the Father. Send the Love and Light to Mother Earth, that in the new dimension she may be restored to her former beauty and you may dwell there in Love, a Paradise of Love for all, as the Father decreed. There you will indeed express the Life Abundant, according to the Father's Will, the Life He holds out to all His Children.

The material goods you have gathered will perish and leave you with nothing. The Father's Love is eternal and, with His Grace, will supply you with treasure beyond human understanding, which will never perish.

Prepare yourselves for the Realms of Light, my brothers, my sisters. Let the Light fill you and Love unlimited come forth from you to all that is in life.

The Blessing and the Love of the Father be upon you now and always. Amen, Amin, Amen, Shalom

XXXV

He said "Let there be Light in your Being. Darkness is not for you. You are Children of Light, and the Light must come forth and set the Universe ablaze with Love. There is no power that can stop Love. Love is the Supreme Power for Love is God. Let your Love be pure and holy, that you see all your brothers and sisters as the Children of Light they are.

As your planet ascends into the new dimension, Love must uphold and sustain it. The Power of Love, the Power of the Father, is the energy of the planet. Without Love the planet will fail and all its beauty will disappear. Your Love must cleanse the planet of the darkness that seeks to destroy it. Your Love must open the Path of Peace and Wholeness. Take to your heart every one of your brothers and sisters, every part of the Father's Creation. Enfold them in your arms. Protect them with your Strength. Let your Wisdom show the Way of Light, so that you and every aspect of Planet Earth may be lifted to the Heights of Glory."

Love and Light. Love and Light. The Way of the Masters, the Way for you, for your brothers and sisters, for the animals, the plants, the flowers, the oceans, the seas and the rivers. Let Peace, the Peace of the Father, fill your Being, the Peace that transcends all earthly thought.

We are here to spiritualize our Earth, that it and we may ascend to the Father's glorious Kingdom. Therefore, my beloved ones, take up your mission. Walk in the Light, the Light of Love, and all will be well.

As it was in the beginning, is now and ever shall be. Glory unto the Father and to His Creation, in the name of Love.

So mote it be.

XXXVI

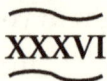

The Father speaks, but Man hears Him not. The Father speaks, but Man heeds Him not. The Words of the Father are planted in the heart and mind and soul of Man, words of Love, of Wisdom, of the Perfectability of All, but Man still languishes in hate, in greed, in neglect of his fellow beings because he neither hears nor heeds. He deals with the intellect only, the shallow empty things, and eats not at the Table of Wisdom, where he might receive the most profound truths, the truths that will cause him never to hunger or thirst again.

O beloved of the Father, come to His Table of Love and Wisdom. There eat of the Truth that shall set you free. Do you not desire freedom from hunger, from doubt, from fear? Do you not thirst for the Wisdom that shall set that Truth before you? Do you not desire the Light that shall bring you face to face with the Father, with His all-encompassing Love? You cannot, in your heart of hearts, prefer the ugliness of the Darkness when the beauty of the Light is before you.

Turn from the Darkness. Cast out doubt and fear. Let go of greed and hatred. Turn to your fellowman in Compassion, in Love, in Kindness. You are all Children of Love and Light, and if you would only see the glories of Love and Light, your world would become a place of such beauty and joy, of such wonder and rejoicing that human words cannot describe.

To achieve this state of being listen to and hear the words of the Galilean … "Thou shalt love the Lord thy God with all of thy mind, and with all of thy heart and with all of thy soul." "Thou shalt love thy neighbor as thyself." "Have ye love one for another."

Where there is Love, where there is Light, hate, greed, envy, jealousy cannot function nor survive. In a world of Love and Light all men are accepted as equals; every man, woman and child is cared for and given love and well-being. There is plenty for all, and none need cheat or hurt his neighbor. As all are One in the Father, any who harm their neighbors are also harming themselves and seeking to harm the Father.

But this need not be. Seek rather that Perfect and Glorious Kingdom of the Father. Seek all that is expressed in the Father's Love and Wisdom, the Paradise that He has created for you, and you will lack nothing. You are His Child, He your Loving Father.

Hear and heed Him, and enter into your Kingdom.

Hallelujah sing the Angel Choirs. Now, let Earth and its peoples reply Hallelujah, our God is with us. The Love and Blessing of the Father be known to you now and always. Amen

XXXVII

God said "Let there be Light", and there was Light, the glorious Light of the Father, that shone upon Man and the Earth. But Man turned his back on the Light, choosing the Darkness instead, because in the depths of his being he did not want his thoughts or his actions revealed by the Light.

And now the Father has intensified that Light, filling it with His Love, His Wisdom, His Grace. He offers again to Man His glorious Kingdom, where Man may know Love, the greatest Love of all. In that Love is everything the Father offers His Children so that they may never hunger or thirst again, may never know want, lack of Love and Understanding; where His Hand will always guide and protect them, His Grace will be their complete fulfilling and supply. In that Kingdom all is Love and rejoicing, all is Peace everlasting.

The Father does not condemn past sins that are repented. He asks only that His Children turn back to Him and accept His Love and His Peace, that they turn again to the Light, letting that Light lead them to Love of all His Creation.

Turn back to the Light, my beloved ones, that you may know the Joy of the Father's Kingdom. Put aside your greed, your hate, your envy and jealousy, and welcome into your heart all your brothers and sisters, every loved and loving manifestation of the Father's Creation of Love.

What has your life in the Darkness brought you? What do you know but pain, anxiety and worry? Why have you brought upon yourselves a world in which brother kills brother, where neighbors – your brothers and sisters – are killed for empty reasons? Why do you enter into war after war with peoples who do not see life as you do?

Dear Ones, put down your weapons, end your killings, and think with Love of all who inhabit your planet. The time is fast approaching when the Earth on which you dwell will be moving into a new dimension, but only those who turn to the Light, who see nothing but Love, will go with Mother Earth. Those who choose the Darkness will remain in an ever-increasing darkness, and great will be their despair and sorrow.

Come, my loved ones, it is the Father's pleasure to give you His Kingdom, His Love, His Grace. Raise your eyes to the Light and follow the Path of Love it reveals. Join hands with your brothers and sisters in Love; let your Love be given to the animals of Earth, the flowers, the plants, to everything and everyone in God's Creation, and the great Shining City of Love will be your abode.

Love, Love, Love. Love is the Door. Open it and all God's Kingdom shall be yours.

I bless you with all my Love. Peace and Love be yours now and forevermore.

Shalom, Salaam, Amin, Amen

XXXVIII

I asked what I should write now, and he said write of the Father's Love for His Children, write of His wish that every child of His heart should know Joy, Happiness and pure Love. Write that He asks each child to accept the gift of the Father's Love and Care; that each child may truly experience the Supreme Joy of knowing that the Father, the Christ of the Father, dwells with and within them.

There is no end to the Father's Love. His Light encompasses all His Creation. If Man would but realize and accept this Love, this Light, he would dwell eternally in Paradise.

The time has come for the choice to be made – Light and Love or Darkness and negativity. As Mother Earth prepares herself for her coming Ascension into her new dimension, all of the Father's Children must choose whether to make that Ascension with her or to remain in the Darkness they have created for themselves.

Choose, my beloved ones, choose. Accept the gifts of the Father's Light and Love. The Darkness can avail you nothing of Life, can give you only brief non-lasting shallow happiness. But out of the Father's Light and Love come abundance of Life, Joy without ceasing and true everlasting Happiness in the Father's Kingdom. Can it be so difficult to make the choice? The Father holds out His Arms to you and bids you come, bids you accept the Kingdom that awaits you. Light, Love, Life are yours for the asking. In the Name and Love of the Father, choose wisely my children. The Father will not impose a choice upon you. The choice can only be made by your free will, but, my dearest ones, for your own sakes choose well and wisely, for the consequences of your choice will remain with you for time immeasurable.

XXXIX

The long night is past. See the Light of Lights where the Dawn is breaking. The Light of the Father shines upon His Children, and welcomes them to the New World which He has created – a New World of Peace, of Love, of Brotherhood.

Let there be no more wars, but only the Joy of Peace; no more hatred, but only the Joy of Brotherhood and Love. Brother take the hand of brother, sister support sister, and all join the Circle of Love the world was designed to be.

In this New World will be no more racial hatred, no more stigmas of birth, no more anger against those who are different. You are all One, One of the Family of God, One with Him and One with each other. Now is the time to turn your spears into ploughshares, to put aside all weapons of destruction and use only the tools of Peace and Love.

What are these tools? Love of the Father, Love of your neighbor, Love of your earth and all the denizens thereof, Love of the fields and meadows, Love of the hills, the mountains, the lakes, the oceans. Love, Peace, Joy, Harmony one with another, that the Earth on which you dwell may be the wondrous place the Father planned and designed. Have you not had enough of hate and destruction? Surely you have, for the Father has opened your eyes and unstopped your ears so that now you hear the sweet music of Love and Peace and now you see the Glorious Light flooding over your New World.

These words are about how to achieve this new creation, how to put aside your truck with the dark forces. Your Brethren from other peaceful planets in the Universe stand ready to help you. Some are among you already. Some are already communicating with those who are open to receive. Many more await the time when they shall stand before you, embracing you in Love and Peace, and showing you, from their Wisdom, how best to bring about a Heavenly Kingdom on your planet.

I, Gezala, will tell of the Way before you; will pour forth my Love to you and give you the guidance that will prepare you for what is ahead.

Glory to the Father of All. His Peace and Love be upon you always.

Amen, Amen, Amen

XL

And now the time approaches. All over this planet of yours landing fields are being prepared for the coming of your brothers and sisters from the Cosmos, from the other planets that God created. But fear not, My Children, they come in Love and Peace to aid you as your Earth is cleansed and makes its Ascension into the Fourth and Fifth Dimensions. They bring you the Wisdom they have learned in the Realms of Light through many millennia. They bring you the Peace that has enabled that Wisdom to grow, and they bring you the Love that is born in Wisdom and Peace.

Many of them are among you already, and have been watching over you and protecting you from the Powers of Darkness. And now those dark powers are weakening. They are being swept from the Earth as the Power of Light faces them and erases them from the knowledge of Men.

Let your hearts be filled with Joy, for the long-promised millennium of fulfillment approaches.

How shall you meet and know these your Brethren? Without fear and filled with thankfulness and Love. Some you will recognize from past incarnations when you were together; others you will know from the Light that shines around them and the sense of Love and Peace that emanates from them. They will bring you tidings of great joy. They will teach and train you in ways to maintain the health and perfection of your bodies as the new energies encompass the Earth. You will feel lighter, freer and more joyous. They will teach you how to change your eating habits as the new vibrations make it necessary for you to do so. They will show you new ways of meditation that will align you with these new lighter, swifter vibrations.

Be ready, My Children. Look to the skies and see the Light. All is Peace and Harmony. Nothing can harm you, for you are fully protected by the Father and these your Brethren.

Lift up your hearts and rejoice, for soon you shall see and be part of the Shining City on the Hill, the New Jerusalem, the Place of Peace. Be ready and greet your Brethren with Love and open arms. They are the salvation promised you from the beginning. Welcome them, Love them, and take your place in the Eden of the Earth.

And so it will be, and so it is, from Him who created all, and now raises His Children to the Height of Heights, for their great Joy and Well-Being.

Shalom, Shalom, Amen

XLI

Children, Children, why are you afraid of your brothers and sisters simply because they come from another planet? Are you not even now planning to land on the Planet Mars if you can? Do you think the people of Mars are in fear of you? Oh no, My Children, they would meet you with Love and a welcome.

Your society has been founded on fear and envy for so many years. You are suspicious of anyone whose skin is different, whose culture is different, whose spiritual worship is different.

Why is "different" not acceptable to you? Have you forgotten that every being on Planet Earth, like every being on every planet in the Universe, is a Child of God, that you all share the same loving Father?

You have allowed your minds to be warped and twisted by the sensational products of the place you call Hollywood. Nothing could be further from the truth than the sensationalism they espouse for financial reasons, for profit.

The Father's Children on His other planets have gone far in understanding the Father's Plan. They know that the energy the Father sends forth is Boundless Love for all He has created – every plant, every flower, every animal and every person is a recipient of that Love if they would but open themselves to it.

And the Father's Children who are already living among you and those who await His Call to come to your aid are as filled with Love as He is. They know the Joy the Ascension of Mother Earth will bring you, and are eager to help you come into that Joy.

I urge you to look for them, to welcome them now in your hearts so they will know they will be welcomed when they come to you. Even now their Lights are beginning to appear in the sky, and soon more and more will be seen.

A New World is even now in its birth pangs, and as the New Dawn draws nearer the birth cry of Joy will be heard.

Evil men have held you in thrall for many millennia, but their time is drawing short. In the new dimensions brother will grasp the hand of brother, sister will help sister as need becomes clear. The Earth will be restored to its intended glory; the very air will hum with Love and the word 'hate' will no longer be known in your language.

The bounty the Father has for His Children will be shared by all in equal measure. People will no longer be judged by their wealth or their status, but by how they express Love, how they help their brothers, how they care for the land for the benefit of all.

And this Utopia will be helped into existence by the very Beings Hollywood has taught you to fear.

My Children, put that fear away from you; fill yourselves with Love and be ready to welcome with that Love those who come to your aid in Love.

The Father bless and keep you as He has from the beginning, does now and shall for evermore. Amen, Amin, Amen

XLII

Have you heard the Word of the Lord? Does His Voice ring in your ears? Then, My Children, hear and obey.

The Word of the Lord is Love and Truth. Therefore, my dear ones, speak only Love and Truth.

Let not darkness nor discord color your speaking. Speak the Word of the Lord that the desert may flower and all distress be swept away.

Let your voice be heard that Men may be drawn unto the Father and the words of your mouth be His.

Let Love and Truth be your watchword now and always.

Beloved, be thou true in His Name. He is with you as you are with Him and never shall you be separated.

Rejoice in the Lord and bear His Banner forth to drive away the Darkness. Look how brightly shines His Light. Be thou His standard-bearer and live in His Light. It is yours for evermore.

XLIII

Love and Light, Light and Love – the Words of the Father. What are these Words? They are the foundation of the Perfect World the Father created. But His Children have chosen instead darkness and hate. And what has this choice produced? What kind of world has it brought about? Look around you, My Children, and what do you see?

You see brother killing brother, nation killing nation. You see disease, poverty, want, cruelty, rapaciousness and anger.

Is this the world you want? Would you not rather see brothers walking hand in hand, nations at peace with each other, health, plenty for all and Love guiding and keeping your world? Would you not rather be able to walk in peace wherever you go? Would you not rather know all the benefits and wonders of the Father's Love and see His Light shine forth upon you?

Then, dear ones, raise and awaken yourselves. Remember you are the Father's Children, His Messengers, His Earthly Self. Remember He is the Presence within you, clearing all the darkness from your Being and filling you with His Light. Prepare yourselves to receive the Love and aid from your brothers and sisters in every part of Creation. Hold out your hands to them in Peace. Open your hearts to them, filled with the Love of the Father. Together you will cleanse your planet of the darkness and hatred, of its envy and anger, and see it take its place in the Paradise your Father created for all His Children.

A Perfected Earth awaits you if you will do your part. And were you not told long ago how to do that? Remember the words: "Have ye Love one for another", "Love your neighbor as yourself". This, my dear ones, is the key that will open the door to Perfection, that will free you and all the Father's Children from hunger, from want, from anger and from hatred.

The Perfect Earth awaits you. Set your feet on the Lighted Path and walk towards the Father. He awaits you all with open arms, ready to give you His Glorious Kingdom and His Eternal Love.

Now is the hour to set your feet on that Path, hand in hand with your brothers and sisters. Go forth in Love and Light to your

Perfection. Be thou whole and One with Him who is all-in-all, now and forever.

God is with you. Be thou with Him.

Amen, Amin, Shalom, Salaam. Hallelujah, Hallelujah, Hallelujah.

Rejoice in Him.

XLIV

How can you not know the Father's Love? It is all around you. It sustains you in time of trouble. It rejoices with you in times of Peace. It brings to you the wondrousness of all the Father is.

And think you this Love is for you alone? Oh no, My Children, it is for every aspect of the Father's Creation – for plants, for flowers, for trees, for oceans, for mountains, for still lakes and small hamlets, for the animals of the field and the wild. But above all it is for Man, Man in all his cultures, all his colors, all his ways. Nor is it for Man of Earth alone. The Father gives His Love to the peoples of all the planets, all the universes in His Creation. And He asks them to give back that Love to each and every one of His Children, wherever in His Creation they may abide.

Great changes are underway on Mother Earth and, because of their Universal Love, the peoples of the galaxies will be joining their Earth brothers and sisters to defeat the Powers of Darkness. The great battle will soon be joined, and the People of the Earth must welcome their brothers and sisters who come to help them. They come from their homes in the galaxies in Love; they do not seek to harm or destroy their Earthly brothers and sisters. Their only enemies are the Powers of Darkness, and against the Light they will bring the Darkness cannot stand. With their help a new and glorious Earth will arise. It will ascend into the Fourth Dimension where war and hatred, greed and envy will not survive. All will be Love and Peace for the Father's Children, and great will be their Joy thereof.

Come, my beloved ones, greet your Brethren in Love, lend your hand and join them in this great endeavor. Be thou One with all that is, so that the Father's Plan may be fully established and your life be a blessing of Joy.

Give praise unto the Father for all He has prepared for you, and rejoice in Him and in His Love, now and always.

His Blessing be upon you. His Love sustain and keep you, and His Wisdom fill you unto all eternity.

And so it is, as it was in the beginning and evermore shall be. Amen, Shalom

XLV

The Light shines forth upon all the Father's Children, awakening them from the Darkness and calling them forth. Come out of your hiding, leave your caves of darkness, leave the dens of blackness and come into the Light. See, it shines for you all, to remind you that you are One with the Father, who is the Light. And in your Oneness, you are the Light too. It is for you to shed the Light of the Father upon the Earth, upon every other planet site in the Universe. Your brothers and sisters of the galaxies know the Light and seek to share it with you, until all Creation is aglow with this wondrous Light.

Does the darkness still hold you? You must make the decision to let it go because it is not for you. You are a Child of Light. Stand forth in its rays and show all who see you that you are Light. It has been said: "If we walk in the Light, as He is the Light, we have fellowship one with another." And from this springs "Have ye Love one for another", because how can you have fellowship without Love. Love and Light, the two great powers of the Father.

Let Love so Light your world that the darkness cannot stand it and flees away. Brotherhood of Love and Light – the true Creation of the Father. All who live and have their being within His Creation are brothers and sisters, One in Him and in each other.

For this was the Universe created, that all, from whatever planet in the Universe, should recognize their Oneness in each other and in Him. It is time for the wars to cease, for the hatred to be turned to Love, for envy, jealousy and greed to be wiped out once and for all.

Join hands with your brothers and sisters from the other planets that a New and Loving Earth may come into full creation. Let Love rule your hearts and all your thoughts, that a true Paradise filled with the Father's Love and Light may be your perfect dwelling place, now and forever.

The Father's Love and Blessing be upon you through all eternity. Shalom, Amen

XLVI

Silence, the Great Silence. What does it mean to you? Do you hear it as nothingness or do you know that it bears the Father's

Voice? In Silence He speaks. His still small voice of Love is in the Silence when He speaks to His Children of Light, who know Him as He knows them. His Love He gives to them in the Silence, assuring them that He and they are One, that the Love between them is eternal, that He will never leave them nor forsake them.

And what do the children of darkness hear? They hear the thunder of His Voice as He chides them for their adherence to the Darkness. But if they listen closely they can also hear the still small voice of Love calling them to Him, that their darkness may be erased and they too can dwell in the Light of His Love.

Which voice do you hear, dear ones? Listen, listen, listen to the Silence which the thunder cannot drown. Listen to the Voice of Love and answer: "Father, here am I. Take me into your arms and let your Light cleanse me, that I may truly serve you, my brothers and sisters, and all Your Children".

The choice is yours, dear ones. For your own sakes, make the right choice and come unto Him, who waits to receive you in Love. Blessed be. Amen

XLVII

Come unto Him all ye that labor. He has promised you rest, a Light burden and an easy yoke. In Him you have Peace and Rest. In Him you have Love and Joy. In Him you have Wisdom and Understanding.

Through Him all Wisdom is yours. It is given to you to know all there is to know that will make your burden Light and your yoke easy.

All the Wisdom of the ages is yours for the asking. Ask and the Akashic Records will be open to you, and you shall stumble in darkness no more. The Light of Lights will illumine your path. All pain will be taken away from you and all Peace and Joy be given unto you.

And what is the price you pay for this? To Love and help your neighbor, to give help to all in need, to speak words of Love to the depressed, to heal the sick and give comfort to those who make the transition from the earth plane. Surely a small price for all the great riches that are awaiting you.

The Darkness knows it is losing the battle with the Light, and in its death throes its wickedness is increasing. This cannot prevail. The Sons of Light are joined in unity, wherever their dwelling place may be, to end the travails set by Darkness. Lift up your heads, My Children, and see the Light. Bathe in it and wash away all the darkness from your Being. Fill yourself with it and know who you are. Stand forth as a Child of the Father and proclaim the Day of Love and Light. Stretch out your hands in welcome to every bringer of that Light to the Earth, and rejoice that you are One with them, with the Father and all that is.

The New Heaven and the New Earth is a-borning, and great shall be that birth. Great shall be the Joy, the Peace, the Wisdom and the Love that surrounds that birth, and all Creation shall give thanks to its Creator and call Him Blessed.

And, my dear ones, know that you are counted among the Blessed and give thanks that you shall know no pain, no sorrow, but only Joy and Love eternally, for evermore.

Stand, Children of Light, and be counted among the Father's Army of Peace and Love. Sing aloud the new song of Freedom and Joy, and shout Hosannas to the Father, who has brought forth His wondrous Realm for your habitation.

Now is the hour. Now are the Children of Light ready. Forward in His Name and do His Will. His Hand is over you. Nothing can harm or deter you. He has spoken it, and so it is. Praise be to Him forever.

Amen

XLVIII

Hear me, O Children of the Father. I speak the Words and the Will of the Father. Hear me.

The Father Loves His Children, and His every thought is for their good, their health, their welfare. His Hands are held out in blessings over each and every one, and He awaits their realization that in Him they find Peace and Rest. He awaits their acknowledgement of His Thought and Guidance that He sends forth to each and every one of His Children.

What is your life without His Love and Wisdom? What is your life if you do not share that Love and Wisdom with your brothers and sisters? What is your life if you turn in fear from your Brethren of the far galaxies? They look to you in Love. They look to help you rid the Earth of Darkness and the People of Darkness who seek to enslave you. You and your Brethren are all Children of the Light and abhor the Darkness. Look to your Brethren in this hour as Mother Earth is cleansed for her Ascension. They it is who are beaming Light and Love to you, strengthening your resolve, helping you to be more aware of the Light. You have nothing to fear from them. They are your kin. Know you not that you first came from the places of their dwelling? You and they are One in the Father, and their only thought is to help you, Love you and clear your way to the heavenly freedom the Father holds in His hands for you.

In the togetherness they offer you is the foundation of the New Jerusalem. Open your hearts to them and accept their Love. Soon they will be among you. Look to the skies and you will see them come, in Love, in Peace, in the Beauty of the Father.

All is well, beloved, all is well. One Earth, One Heaven, One Family of the Father. Rejoice and be exceeding glad. All glory is before you in Love and Light for evermore.

Glory be to all the Father's Children, Glory be to the Father, the Son and the Holy Spirit, now and forever more. Amen.

Hallelujah, Hallelujah, Hallelujah. And so it is.

XLIX

Let your Light so shine that the Darkness, which comprehendeth not the Light, shall flee away and hide itself in the darkest hole, where it will fade into nothingness and be gone forever.

Let your Light so shine that people shall be drawn to it, and it will help them put away all Darkness from their being.

Let your Light so shine that it shall be a beacon to the Brethren who are preparing to come to your aid, to assist in Mother Earth's Ascension. And as that Ascension proceeds, let your Light so shine that all who Love Mother Earth shall see and know that the hour has indeed come when she and all who dwell on her in Light have made their dwelling in the Fourth Dimension, and are already preparing for their next Ascension into the Fifth.

O my dear ones, let the glory of the Father shine in your Light. Let His Love fill all that you are and all that you do. Let your thoughts be filled with that Light that all may know you show forth the Father's Light and Love, and send it forth into every corner, every cranny, every part of the now-Perfecting Earth.

Yours is a glorious task, and the Father, who knows all His Children, has made ready all His Children of Light to take their place in this great battle.

Be not afraid, for victory is sure. The Darkness cannot stand against the Light, although it will try for a little while longer. But stand firm, My Children, and the Light will indeed prevail, and the glorious City of Light will be seen on the Hill, to tell all the Father's Children the Perfected Earth is now their Home, their Earthly Home.

And when their travail is done, an even more glorious Home awaits them, where they may rest from their labors in the Father's Love.

Be bold and steady, My Children. Look to the Light for strength, and all will be well.

The Blessing and Love of the Father be upon you now and always.

I am he, Gezala, who sends you the Father's Word and Love. Be ye faithful unto Him now and always. Amen, Amin, Shalom

≈
L
≈

Write, child, write. Write of the New Earth which is now being formed. Write of its manifestation as Man learns to listen to the Words of the Father, as Man learns to put aside forever the things that have kept him from clear communion with the Father.

The time approaches when all Mankind, all the Father's Creation shall know they are One with and in Him and each other. Put aside the old things and look to the new – the New Jerusalem, the new loving communion with the Father, the new love and acceptance of every aspect of the Father's Creation.

Look for old friends, those you have loved and admired from this and previous incarnations. They and you are to be united again as the Father's New Earth comes into being. You will know and recognize each other, and an even greater love and comradeship will bloom between you. Those you have long missed will stand before you again, in a different guise, yes, but you will know each other, and great will be the joy between you as you clasp hands again.

And why is this happening? Because the great love that will spring up from these meetings will set a foundation that will establish the New Earth of Love and Light. As Love builds on Love, the New Earth will be manifested. Its beauty will be beyond anything you have yet seen on your planet. Flowers and trees more glorious, rivers and lakes sparkling with Light, animals of great beauty expressing greater Love and, yes, speaking to you in words you can understand.

And what of Man himself? Your brothers and sisters will shine in a great beauty that springs from the Godhead itself. Love will shine from their eyes, their actions will express the Love of the Father, and all will be peaceful and joyous in the Garden of the New Earth.

Are you ready to do your part, dear ones? Are you ready to live in Love and Peace, to put aside hate, anger, greed, envy, all things not of the Father? My beloved ones, hear the call and prepare yourselves. Make ready for the Eden of the New Earth by harboring only thoughts of Love and Peace, by holding out helping hands to your brothers and sisters in need and, above all, Loving the Father with all of your mind, with all of your heart and with all of your soul.

His is Creation and all that is therein. Be ready to be a living part of it in Light and Love.

Blessings and Love be upon you now and always. And so it is.

LI

In the Halls of the Father is our dwelling place. There we shall know Peace, Love, Plenty and wondrous Beauty. There no wars will be known, no hatred, no envy, no greed. Each Child of the Father shall know the great pleasure of sharing with his brothers and sisters – sharing Love, sharing Wisdom and all Knowledge that the Father will open to each Child. In the act of sharing shall great Joy be known and each and every one shall live and have his Being in that Joy.

But, my beloved, there is much work to be done that we may reach that Joy. Darkness and the Dark Powers must be swept away, out of existence. The Earth must be flooded with the Light of Lights, that no dark corner may remain.

And who is to do this work? Why, who but you, my dear ones, who but you? This is your mission, this is the fulfilling of your pre-birth contract with the Father. This is why your brothers and sisters of the galaxies are standing by to help you with this task. And, as we have said before, you have been given the greatest weapon in the Father's Armory to do this work, and you know what that weapon is, do you not? Yes, you know that it is Love, the greatest and most powerful weapon there is. Therefore, dear ones, in every moment of the life you are now experiencing, send forth that Love to your brothers and sisters wherever they may be, to every living thing on your planet, to everyone dwelling in the Father's great galaxies, to every aspect of the Cosmos. The Darkness, the Dark Powers, cannot abide the wondrous power of Love. They shrink from it in pain and despair, in hatred and anger. Let your Love be Light. Let your Love fill all your Being, that you may be in the forefront of the battle that will destroy the Darkness forever.

Behold, the Light has come again and seeks to encompass and fill you, giving you its protection, giving you Peace and Joy everlasting. Welcome it, my beloved ones, and give all your aid to Mother Earth as she makes her Ascension. The Father and all the Beings of Light await you, and great shall be your future and that of all the Children of Light.

Hasten, for the hour is close at hand, and the Father looks to you to aid His Victory, which shall be unto everlasting.

Glory to the Father and all His Glorious Kingdom, now and forever more. Amen, Amin, Amen. Alleluia, Alleluia, Alleluia

LII

Stand up, ye Children of the Light. Stand and declare your allegiance to the Father's Light and His Love. Put on the whole armor of the Father and stand in His Name against the Forces of Darkness.

Let your hearts be strong, for though there is a final battle ahead, the Darkness cannot win, and Mother Earth shall make her Ascension into the Light of Lights, into the dimension of Victory.

Your inter-galactic Brethren stand at your side to give you their aid. St. Michael has drawn his Sword of Truth and leads the Angelic Host in your aid. Be strong, My Children. Make the choice to put the Darkness from you. Shine the Father's Light into every nook and cranny of your Being. Make sure no dark thoughts remain in your heart and mind. Think and know only Love and Light, fellowship with all and everything in the Father's Creation. His Glorious Kingdom, the Kingdom of Love and Light, is yours here and now, as the Darkness is driven from every part of His Creation.

Did you think you had to experience so-called Death to enter that Kingdom? Not so, my dearly beloved. If you live in the Father's Love and Light that Kingdom can be yours now, as you continue your present earthly incarnation. That Kingdom is built of Love, and you will know it is yours, all of Love is yours, all who Love are yours, if you know and accept nothing but Love. No, I am not the first to present these words to you. They were said many millennia ago, but they still convey the great Truth of the Father.

Give forth your Love to all, whether you know them, whether you only know of them, or whether they are strangers to you.

They are all One in the Father, and in you. Was it not said long ago: "Succor the stranger at your gate; you may be entertaining an Angel unawares"?

Yes, you are an Angel, and so is every Being of Light in the Father's Kingdom. Remember that always, my beloved ones, and do the Father's Will in that knowledge. Thus will the Gates of the Kingdom be opened unto you.

Walk through those Gates, dear ones, and walk in the glorious paths of the Kingdom, now and always.

Peace be unto you, and the Light of Lights guide you, now and forever more. Amin, Amen in Love.

LIII

Why does Man hesitate in the Darkness? Look how brightly the Light shines. Look how beautiful is everything upon which the Light shines. Beauty brings such Joy to Mankind's soul, and yet he finds it difficult to give up the things of Darkness that bring brief shallow pleasure.

How much more abundant, how much more satisfying and eternal are the pleasures of the things of Light.

Has not your heart lifted at the sight of a beautiful sunrise or sunset? Does not your heart leap for joy at the sound of a bird's song or a beautiful chorale? Do you not rejoice at reading magnificent words of poetry and great literature? Why then do you choose to turn back to the Darkness, which gives you nothing lasting?

Dear ones, it is time to make your final choice, to take up the Light burden and put your hand to the Plough of Peace.

Nothing in your life can be more beautiful, more everlasting than the Victory you can aid in the battle between the Darkness and the Light. Nothing can give you more lasting Joy than to work with the Light to ensure Mother Earth's Ascension. Do you not understand what awaits you after the Victory over the Powers of Darkness? How often have you been told: "It is your Father's pleasure to give you the Kingdom" and "Seek ye first this Kingdom, and all else shall be added unto you"?

How glorious are the paths of the Kingdom of Light and Love. How peaceful are the dwellings thereof. How wondrous is the Love and Joy that will fill you there.

Why then do you hesitate? Do you fear you must leave this incarnation to enter the Kingdom? No, My Children, no. The Kingdom is here for you now. You can enter its Gates today if you are prepared to live in Light and Love, if you are prepared to accept all your brothers and sisters, whoever and wherever they may be, as One with you; if you are prepared to nurture the planet the Father has given you, prepared to love and care for the animals that co-habit the planet with you.

This is no difficult choice, beloved, if you accept that all the Father's Kingdom and all its inhabitants are One with each other and with the Father.

Wash yourselves in the Waters of Life, and cleanse your Being of all Darkness. Rejoice in the Light and the Love it brings to you, and enter your Kingdom of Love and Light now.

All blessings be upon you now and always.

Amen, Amin, Shalom, Salaam

LIV

Can you hear the Silence? Can you hear the Father's Voice in that Silence? Listen, dear ones, listen. Hear the Love He gives you in the Silence, the Love that is yours to send forth into all Creation – the Love that enables you to forgive your enemies and do good to those who despitefully use you.

Forgive, dear ones, forgive and Love. And first forgive yourselves. Remember you are One with the Father, but the Father knows that you set your expectations far ahead, into realms you are not yet ready to enter. Step by step, My Children, step by step. It takes a little longer sometimes than you would wish to perfect each aspect of your Being, the Being that must be perfected if you wish to aid the Ascension of Mother Earth, and if you wish to accompany that Ascension. All will be perfected, but in the Father's time. Each step along the way brings you closer to that perfection if you listen to the Father and take heed of what He tells you.

Remember too that you are all walking to the same place, the Father's Perfect Kingdom, but each of you has a different route to that wondrous place. The Father does not "play favorites", for you are all favored and He sets you on the path that is best for each of you. You all have different karma to resolve, you all have different errors to correct, so of course your paths are different. But, dear ones, imagine the Joy that will be yours when you achieve the goal the Father has set you.

Be strong, therefore, as you walk, knowing always that all the Father's Perfect Kingdom is yours here and now, on Mother Earth

Be content to make your journey as you planned with the Father as you set your pre-birth contract. Listen to His Voice in the Silence, and know He is always with you, always fills you with His Love and guides you with His Wisdom.

All Joy, Peace and Blessing, filled with the Father's Love, be yours now and always. And so it is.

LV

Come unto the Source who created you, gave you and your brothers and sisters the Earth and all the galaxies in which to live and have your Being. Above all, He gave you Light to fill you with Love to enable the Christ to be formed in you. The Nazarene long ago told you not to marvel at the things He did, for you were destined to do greater things.

The Light shines in the Darkness, causing the Powers of Darkness to cower in their dark holes, drawing away from the Light, sent to annihilate their dark works. The time fast approaches, Beloved, when the Darkness shall finally be finished, eradicated entirely from the places whereon you dwell. A thousand million millennia of Light Perfected Earth, peopled by the Father's Light bearers, are before you. Peace beyond present understanding shall fill your dwelling places. Joy beyond compare shall be yours for evermore. Love, the Love of the Christ-bearers, shall fill your hearts and minds. There shall be none you call enemy, for the time of Brotherhood shall be yours. Brother shall clasp brother, sister shall be one with all sisters, and great shall be the World of Heaven.

A paradise is before you, but you must do your part. Hold out your hand in friendship to all who come to you asking for help. Bind up the wounds of those in pain, and give them Peace. Let Love be your watchword as you gather all into the Light.

Now is the time, My Children, to put away the things of Darkness and dwell only in the Light. Light you are as the Father is Light. Love you are as He is Love. He has chosen you, and you have consented to carry out this mission of perfecting Mother Earth. Long has she known the anguish of seeing her trees and forests destroyed, species after species of her animal kingdom eliminated, her oceans, seas, rivers and lakes polluted, and she has called on all to change this state and renew the Earth and all Creation to its initial beauty. When the Father created the Universe He pronounced it to be good. Man has almost destroyed the goodness, but now has the opportunity to restore it, to make all Creation a Second Eden.

Come unto the Light, dear ones, and take your stand against the Darkness, that the Father's Creation may again be pronounced good.

The Light is with you, the Angelic Beings are with you, as are your Brothers and Sisters of the Galaxies. Join them in this great work, and rejoice in the Father's Love, now and always.

His Blessing, His Love and His Presence are with you always. Hallelujah, Emmanuel is with us. Shalom, Salaam, Amen, Amin

LVI

All hail to the Light of Lights! It shines upon Mother Earth to aid her in her Ascension. It shines upon you to aid you to rise with her into the Perfected Earth.

O My Children, look to the Light. Look to the Joy within its rays, look to the absence of pain it brings. Look to the Wisdom, the Strength, the Peace, the Love.

How has Man lived so long in Darkness? It has weakened his wisdom, his ability to love and sustain his brothers and sisters, and has made life seem so long and unclear.

But that is now ended. The Light brings new hope and happiness beyond anything you have known.

Life will be open. All will know all things the Father wants Man to understand – the Beauty of being One with all Creation, on Earth and beyond. Your Brothers and Sisters of the Galaxies will bring you brotherhood not previously known to you. They will join with you in perfecting the Earth. They will aid you in deepening your understanding, and show you wonders beyond anything you have yet seen.

Dear ones, they are your friends and your teachers. They have walked the path that is now before you, and can pass on to you the lessons they have learned along the way. They can show you ways to make your burdens Light, to put the Darkness from you and to walk in Peace and Joy, singing songs of praise to the Father in great lightheartedness.

So much is before you, My Children, so much Love, so much Joy, so much Brotherhood and Peace between all nations and peoples.

Lift up your hearts and your voices in welcome to those who come in Love to aid you, and the road will, as your saying is, rise to meet you. Your road will be filled with gladness and harmony and with songs of Joy. Former enemies will greet you as friends.

Loved ones who went on ahead of you will join you as you walk, and great will be the rejoicing between you.

Now is the time for great Faith. Sometimes it will seem to you that only danger and harm are around you. But, beloved, your Faith will keep you whole. Much cleansing of the Darkness that filled the Earth is taking place, and this must be done that Mother Earth may make her Ascension. The great teacher Isaiah said long ago: "They that wait upon the Lord shall renew their strength; they shall mount up with wings as eagles; they shall run, and not be weary; and they shall walk, and not faint." This is your destiny, beloved, this is your Path. Put your Faith into action and wait upon the Lord, and all will be well for you. You shall renew your strength and not be weary; you shall run and not be faint. You shall be the inhabitors of the Perfected Earth and be exceeding glad. His Blessing is upon you and His Love surrounds and fills you, now and forever.

Amen, Amin, Amen

LVII

I have heard the Word of the Lord, the Word that will set you free. Hear me, My Children, as the Word is for you.

The Word, as I have told you many times, is Love, but it would seem that many of you are not prepared to hear or, if you hear, to act on it.

How can so many of Earth's people carry so much hate for so long? Why does nation still strive against nation? Who has set any nation to overwhelm others, to decide how other nations shall live and act?

Only the Father can make such decisions, and the Father's Word is Love, not hate. He it is who set the pattern of the nations. He it is who knows how each of His Children, each of the nations, should act, how they should express their Love and Praise to Him.

Look to yourselves, each of my people. See how your actions result in war, in suffering and distress. Take the beam from your own eye before you ask your brother to remove the mote from his.

The Father desires only Love and Peace for all His Children. Change your unpeaceful ways now, if you wish to leave the Darkness and live in the Light.

Change your hatred to Love if you wish to join Mother Earth as she makes her Ascension into the dimension of Love. As Mother Earth ascends she will eliminate hatred from her Being, she will eliminate anger, suffering and the hurt so many of her people have suffered for so long. All negativity will be wiped from her Being for those who choose to ascend with her. Light shall be her path, Light shall be her way of Life, and the Earth will be infused with a Love that has not been known to Man before.

Seek ye the way of Light and Love, my beloved, that you may know this Peace and Understanding. The Father is with you and desires only that your ways may be pleasant and lovely. Take His Hand and walk with Him in the Paradise to come, that all may be well with you.

Bless you, each and every one who hears my words and obeys. Great Joy lies before you. Give thanks to the Father and accept His Gifts now and always.

God be with you each and every day, as you seek to do His Bidding. And so mote it be. Amen, Amin, Amen

LVIII

Let not your hearts be troubled. The Father is with you always, and His Love and Light fill and surround you. Welcome Him and His Christ into your hearts. The Darkness cannot overwhelm you, for the Angels of Light surround and protect you from all evil.

Lift up your voices rejoicing, for the time of the Perfected Earth approaches. And remember, dear ones, the word Earth does not apply only to the planet on which you live. You and your physical bodies are also the Earth, as the Father is the Heavens. To perfect the Earth you must cleanse from your whole Being – body, emotions, mind and soul – every aspect of the Darkness. Remember the words "though your sins be as scarlet, they shall be as white as snow", through the Love of the Father.

Come into and be of the Light, and wondrous shall be the Earth on which you dwell. Live in the Light and let the Love of the Father pour forth from you to all of His Creation. This is the way the Father desired you to live, but the Powers of Darkness took over and Man accepted them. But their time draws to an end, and the Father's Glorious Light shall wipe away all the sadness and despair those Dark Powers created. Light shall be your lives and great Joy shall fill and move your Being.

You are of the Light, dear ones. Take it into your Being. Live in its rays and never know darkness or despair again.

Your Brothers and Sisters of the Galaxies are poised to help you, to wipe away the Darkness. They already live in the Light, and their Strength and Radiance shall indeed Light your path to the Realms of Light that await you. The call has gone forth, and they are ready to give you all the aid you need. They have great Love for you as their Brothers and Sisters, and eagerly await the Father's command to join you.

The long night is almost over, and the Radiant Day approaches. Be ready, My Children, and welcome that Day in Joy, which shall be yours unto everlasting.

The Peace of the Father, the Blessing of the Father, the Light of the Father and the Love of the Father be with you now and always. So mote it be. Shalom, Salaam. It is done.

LIX

And now, my beloved brothers and sisters, I have done my best through these writings to show you the Way, to turn your hearts, your minds, your souls to the Light, to Love, to your Loving Father. I have also given you my Love and my Wisdom. I have set the course to bring you to awareness of the Father's Love and Wisdom, His Grace and His Strength. Have no fear – I am not leaving you. My Spirit will always be with you.

I love you, I bless you and I look forward with Joy to our new fellowship.

Glory be to the Father and to the Son and to the Holy Spirit, as it was in the beginning, is now and ever shall be.

Now let your voices be raised in praise to Him who was from the beginning and evermore shall be; He who is your Everlasting Father, the Bestower of all Joy, the Giver of Eternal Love and Light.

And so it is, and so it shall be through all eternity. Hallelujah, Hallelujah, Shalom, Salaam, Amen.

I AM he who is Gezala, the Messenger of the Father, now and evermore.

Love and Light, Light and Love to you all.

I Gezala am but the Messenger. the spokesman if you will. I and my nine companions of the Magic Circle are one of the repositories of the Father's Will and Words. What the Father gives to us, we give to you, and because we love you, with the Father's blessing, we add what we have learned through many lifetimes that we may make your journey easier. So many of us here and you now on Earth have been together through many incarnations. We have paid our karmic debts; we have kept our pre-birth commitments, and we of the Magic Circle have now made a new commitment, to be of service to you until you join us here. Therefore, as we now complete this phase of our work, we do so in great Love. As the Galilean said: "A little while I AM with you, and then in a little while I AM not with you, and then in a while I AM with you again." We will always answer when you call on us.

God bless you. Adieu in Love and Grace. Gezala and the Magic Circle.

The Rt. Rev. Carole M. Phelan

Carole Phelan is a teacher, counselor and ordained minister who has long been a proponent of spiritual unfoldment and development. She was educated in England, where she also worked in the British film industry and for one of Britain's oldest and most respected publishing houses. In the 1960's she and her late husband Christopher came to America, where they became active in a Southern California metaphysical church and Christopher became an ordained minister. In the 1970's they established their own church and Carole was ordained in 1975. Carole now resides in Annapolis, Maryland and continues to use her healing and counseling abilities to aid those who seek her help.

To order copies of this book and other books by
Terra Nova Publishing LLC, please visit:

www.terranovapublishingllc.com

9780983778608